unSpun

unSpun

*Finding Facts
in a World of Disinformation*

Brooks Jackson
and **Kathleen Hall Jamieson**

RANDOM HOUSE TRADE PAPERBACKS   NEW YORK

For Beverly and Bob

A Random House Trade Paperback Original

Copyright © 2007 by Brooks Jackson and Kathleen Hall Jamieson

All rights reserved.

Published in the United States by Random House Trade Paperbacks,
an imprint of The Random House Publishing Group,
a division of Random House, Inc., New York.

RANDOM HOUSE TRADE PAPERBACKS and colophon are
trademarks of Random House, Inc.

ISBN 978-1-4000-6566-0

Library of Congress Cataloging-in-Publication Data
Jackson, Brooks.
unSpun : finding facts in a world of disinformation /
by Brooks Jackson and Kathleen Hall Jamieson.
p.   cm.
ISBN 978-1-4000-6566-0
1. Deception—United States.   2. Deceptive advertising—United States.
3. Communication in politics—United States.   4. Truthfulness and
falsehood—United States.   I. Jamieson, Kathleen Hall.   II. Title.
III. Title: Finding facts in a world of disinformation.
BF637.D42J33 2007
177'.3—dc22   2006050437

Printed in the United States of America

www.atrandom.com

1 2 3 4 5 6 7 8 9

Book design by Susan Turner

Contents

Introduction

A World of Spin

WE LIVE IN A WORLD OF SPIN.

It flies at us in the form of misleading commercials for products and political candidates and about public policy matters. It comes from businesses, political leaders, lobbying groups, and political parties. Millions are deceived every day, buying products, voting for candidates, supporting policies and even wars—all because of spin.

"Spin" is a polite word for deception. Spinners mislead by means that range from subtle omissions to outright lies. Spin paints a false picture of reality by bending facts, mischaracterizing the words of others, ignoring or denying crucial evidence, or just "spinning a yarn"—by making things up.

Some degree of spin can be considered harmless, as when a person puts his best foot forward in hopes that we won't notice that the other shoe may be a bit scuffed. But we're not writing here about mere puffery, nor are we criticizing advocates who argue strongly and honestly for their side; we're talking about outright dishonesty, misrepresentation, and a lack of respect for facts. We see these far too commonly today in politics and business alike.

Spin is tolerated and even admired in some circles. In Washington, a good spin doctor is lauded, much like a twenty-game winner in baseball. But we believe voters and consumers need to recognize spin when it is used against them, just as good batters spot the spin on a curveball. If they don't recognize spin, they risk not only buying the wrong cold remedy or the wrong car but also going into the voting booth with false notions in their heads about the candidates.

Spin misleads people about matters as trivial as a jar of beauty cream or as deadly serious as cancer. Readers may find our examples variously outrageous and amusing, but we hope all of them are instructive. Our purpose in writing this book is to give readers some tools for recognizing and avoiding spin, and finding solid facts.

Both parties spin, but we'll start, arbitrarily, with a Republican example. To illustrate what we mean when we say that spin is deception, consider an appearance of Karl Rove, senior adviser to President George W. Bush, at the American Enterprise Institute in Washington, D.C., on May 15, 2006. Rove gave a vigorously upbeat picture of the American economy, and nothing he said was absolutely false, yet the overall impression he tried to create was at times so divorced from reality as to seem unhinged.

Rove said, for example: "Real disposable income has risen almost 14 percent since President Bush took office. The Dow Jones industrial average is near its all-time high. And since the 2003 tax cuts have been passed, asset values, including homes and stocks, have grown by $13 trillion."

All that was true, and a listener might well have concluded that the income of every American had risen. But Rove failed to mention that since Bush took office, poverty had worsened significantly, millions of workers had lost their health insurance, and real wages were stagnant for rank-and-file payroll employees. The "real disposable income" he cited was a statistic that measures the total increase in income, not how that increase is distributed. According to the U.S. Census Bureau, real income (after inflation) for the typical U.S. household had fallen by 3.6 percent during Bush's first four years in office—a loss of $1,670 in 2004 dollars. The income gains of which Rove spoke were going almost exclusively to those in the upper half of society, the same affluent households that owned the stocks, bonds, and expensive homes whose values had grown so dramatically.

Democrats engage in similar behavior. In fact, two weeks after Rove's speech, the U.S. Bureau of Labor Statistics reported that the economy had added another 75,000 jobs in the previous month and that the unemployment rate had dropped to 4.6 percent. And yet the Democratic National Committee called the results "more evidence of President Bush's failed economic record," saying economists had expected a somewhat larger job gain. In fact, the unemployment rate was the lowest in five years, well below the average for all months of the Clinton administration (which was 5.2 percent), and a full percentage point lower than the average for all months since World War II. Thus in the hands of a partisan spinmeister, a better-than-average unemployment rate becomes a failure.

Don't be tempted to dismiss this sort of thing as a mere difference of interpretation or an argument over whether the economic glass is half full or half empty. There is more to it than that. Both sides are actively working to deceive the public. They may even be deceiving themselves to a large degree, and we often see reason to suspect that's the case. Both sides tend to ignore evidence that doesn't favor their point of view and to avoid tough problems by spinning them away and hoping voters won't notice.

We sometimes see this more easily in the world of advertising, where corporate snake-oil salesmen routinely employ spin to get us to buy their products. In this book we'll tell you of an over-the-counter pain reliever that claimed to be "prescription strength" when it was *half* the usual prescription dose, and an Internet service marketed as having "broadband-like speed" when in fact cable modems are several times faster. But as obvious as some advertising deceptions may seem to some of us, they fool any number of people into spending untold hundreds of millions of dollars each year on products that don't perform as advertised. We'll tell you about some well-known products whose sales have been built almost entirely on deception. Advertisers keep spinning because it is profitable to do so.

Spin comes at us today in ways that didn't even exist a decade or so ago. On cable-news talk shows, advocates issue torrents of factual claims daily, seldom challenged by their amiable hosts. And the Internet has enabled a potent new weapon of deception, so-called viral marketing of falsehoods that replicate and spread like a disease. One such message during the 2004 campaign claimed that President Bush secretly planned to reinstitute a military draft if he was reelected. Another claimed that John Kerry's wife was responsible for sending thousands of U.S. jobs overseas. Both were false, but millions of voters believed them. For example, 42 percent of the people we polled immediately after the 2004 election considered it either "somewhat" or "very" truthful that Bush would reinstitute the draft.

We simply can't always count on government regulators, courts, or the news media to sort through the daily barrage of baloney. This book is about how to become *un*spun. We'll explain how to recognize spin, how to understand its nature, and how to spot the techniques spinners use to deceive. We'll show you what years of communications research and advances in human psychology have taught us about why even the most intelligent people are susceptible to being spun. We'll show you how staying unSpun can save your life, not to mention your money and your self-respect.

We'll also show you how, for all the faults of the Internet, you can use it to find reliable information with a few keystrokes, at home, for free, while avoiding misinformation and fraud. And we'll offer some methods for properly weighing and evaluating evidence and reaching your own well-founded conclusions.

We'll share with you the tools that we found useful as we created the Annenberg Public Policy Center's FactCheck.org, a political website designed to be a "consumer advocate" for voters. FactCheck.org got nine million visits during its first two years of operation from citizens seeking help to sort through the deception and confusion in U.S. politics.

A word of caution: if you are a strong partisan just looking to prove the other side is wrong, this book will challenge you to cast the same critical eye on your own beliefs as you do on the other side's. Doing so will not be easy. Research we will introduce later in the book shows that partisans often become accomplices to their own deception by rejecting information, valid or not, merely because it conflicts with their existing beliefs. If you are a bitter cynic who has concluded that nobody is telling the truth, and you have given up looking for facts, we will show you why you don't need to resign yourself to a world of spin.

Avoiding spin and finding solid information can be a challenge, perhaps more than most people realize. Not only are we surrounded by commercial and political pitchmen who are trying their best to pull the wool over our eyes, but also our own brains betray us in ways that psychologists are still struggling to understand. We'll explain how our own biology can blind us to accurate information, and why it is important to work constantly at taking a skeptical approach to advertising and at keeping our minds open to the possibility that, just maybe, the other person has a point.

We hope you'll emerge from this book rightly skeptical of the many dubious claims you read and hear, but willing to consider all the available evidence. We think you *can* tell who's right and who's wrong most of the time, if you are willing to keep an open mind and to put in a bit of effort. And we'll show you how to have some fun doing it.

We take as our motto something the late Senator Daniel Patrick Moynihan of New York was fond of saying: "You are entitled to your opinion. But you are *not* entitled to your own *facts*."

unSpun

Chapter 1

From Snake Oil
to Emu Oil

A CENTURY AGO A SELF-PROCLAIMED COWBOY NAMED CLARK STAN-
ley, calling himself the Rattlesnake King, peddled a product he
called Snake Oil Liniment. He claimed it was "good for man and
beast" and brought immediate relief from "pain and lameness."
Stanley sold it for 50 cents a bottle—the equivalent of more than
$10 today—as a remedy for rheumatism, toothache, sciatica, and
"bites of animals, insects and reptiles," among other ailments. To
promote his pricey cure-all, Stanley publicly slaughtered rattle-
snakes at the Chicago World's Fair of 1893.

Stanley was the most famous of the snake-oil salesmen, back
before passage of the federal Pure Food and Drug Act in 1906. And
he was a fraud. When the federal government finally got around to
seizing some of Stanley's product in 1915, the Department of Agriculture's Bureau of Chemistry (forerunner of today's Food and
Drug Administration) determined that it "consisted principally of a

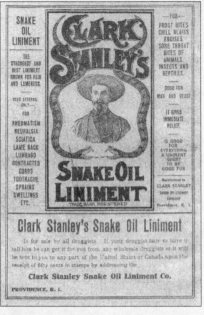

An undated poster, believed to be from around 1905, advertising Clark Stanley's Snake Oil Liniment, which consisted mainly of mineral oil and contained no snake oil at all.

light mineral oil (petroleum product) mixed with about 1 per cent of fatty oil (probably beef fat), capsicum, and possibly a trace of camphor and turpentine." And no actual snake oil. Stanley was charged with violating the federal food and drug act. He didn't contest the charge and was fined $20.

Are today's pitchmen and hucksters any less deceptive? We don't think so. "Snake oil" has a bad name these days (at least in the United States; in China, it is used to relieve joint pain). But in 2006 we found another animal-oil product that—according to its marketer—is "much better than Botox! [and] Makes Wrinkles Almost Invisible to the Naked Eye! . . . Look as much as 20-years younger . . . in less than one minute." The maker even claims that the product won't just hide wrinkles, with repeated use it may eliminate them: "It is possible your wrinkles will no longer even exist." The name of the product is Deception Wrinkle-Cheating Cream. How appropriate.

According to Planet Emu, the marketer, this scientific miracle contains "the only triple-refined emu oil in the world," but we quickly determined that this product is nothing more than triple-refined hokum. Emus are those big, flightless Australian birds; the oil is said to be an ancient Aboriginal remedy. But when we asked Planet Emu for proof of their claims, they cited only one scientific study of emu oil's cosmetic properties, and it had nothing to do with wrinkles. It found that emu oil was rated better than mineral oil as a moisturizer by *eleven* test subjects. We searched the medical literature for ourselves and found some scanty evidence that emu oil may promote healing of burns in rats. We found no testing of emu oil as a wrinkle cream, much less any testing that compared it with Botox.

That's where a century of progress in product promotion has gotten us: from baseless claims for snake oil to baseless claims for emu oil. The products change, but the techniques of deception (small "d") are as underhanded now as they were in the days of Clark Stanley. Meanwhile the price has gone up. "Deception" emu-oil wrinkle cream, at $40 for three quarters of an ounce, costs four times more than a bottle of its snake-oil forebear, even after adjusting for a century of inflation.

Bunk is fairly typical of beauty products. "All the cosmetics companies use basically the same chemicals," a former cosmetics chemist, Heinz J. Eiermann, told *The Washington Post* way back in 1982. "It is all the same quality stuff." Eiermann was then head of the Food and Drug Administration's division of cosmetics technology. His conclusion: "Much of what you pay for is make-believe."

Cosmetics advertising is just one example of the rampant deception that surrounds us. Spin pervades both commerce and politics, and most of it is not so funny. As we'll soon see, any number of products with household names are marketed with false or deceptive advertising. Whole companies have been built on such deception. Elections have been decided by voters who believed false ideas fed to them by manipulative television ads and expressed in "talking points," and if you voted for a presidential candidate in 2004 the odds are you were one of them. The U.S.-led invasion of Iraq wasn't the first American war fought with the passionate support of a public that believed claims about the enemy that turned out to be false.

We've found that whether the spin is political, commercial, or ideological, and whether the stakes are trivial (as with $40 wrinkle remedies) or, quite literally, life and death, the ways by which we are deceived are consistent and not so hard to recognize. The first step in confronting spin is to open our eyes to how often we encounter it. It's so common, so all-pervading, that we can't avoid it.

Prescription-Strength Malarkey

Some examples from commercial advertising:

- Bayer HealthCare once advertised Aleve pain medication as "Prescription Strength Relief Without a Prescription." It wasn't. The maximum recommended dose of Aleve is less than half the usually prescribed dose of Anaprox, a prescription counterpart.

- Munchkin, Inc., said of one of its products: "Baby bottles like Tri-Flow have been clinically shown to reduce colic." But look behind the "clinically proven" claim and you find the test was of a competitor's similar bottle, not Munchkin's.

- NetZero claimed its dial-up Internet service allows users to "surf at broadband-like speeds." It doesn't. Cable modems are several times faster.

- Tropicana claimed in TV ads that drinking two to three glasses a day of its "Healthy Heart" orange juice could reduce the risk of heart disease and stroke. The Federal Trade Commission said those claims weren't supported by scientific evidence, and prohibited the company from repeating the claims in future ads.

Political Snake Oil

Deceptive product promotion is a minor problem compared with political spin. Compare claims for snake oil and emu oil with those routinely made about crude oil—petroleum. In the 2004 presidential campaign, both John Kerry and President George W. Bush spoke to voters of making America "energy independent." Toward the end of the campaign, Professor Robert Mabro, who was then the director of the Oxford Institute for Energy Studies, told *The New Yorker* magazine: "The two candidates, with due respect, are lying to the people, or they don't know what they are talking about."

Our guess is that Bush and Kerry knew exactly what they were talking about. Actually achieving "energy independence" would require huge changes that neither man cared to propose. One independent study, by the Rocky Mountain Institute, projected that the United States could eliminate the need to import any oil from abroad by 2040, if we took such measures as a heavy tax on gas-guzzling vehicles, a federal program to buy and scrap old gas-gulping clunkers, and generous subsidies from taxpayers to help low-income persons buy more fuel-efficient autos. The projected cost of such measures was $180 billion, at least $150 billion more than either Kerry or Bush had pledged, and even so it is probably far too little. Others say that what's required for independence is a government program on the scale of the project that produced the Apollo moon landings.

Sure enough, oil imports continued to rise after Bush was sworn in for a second term, so much that in 2005 the United States imported 59.8 percent of the oil it consumed, up from 58.4 percent in 2004. The increase came despite enactment of a Bush-backed energy bill, which was predicted only to slow the growth of imports modestly, not to reverse it.

The crude-oil spin continues. In his 2006 State of the Union address, the president said the United States was "addicted to oil." But this time he set a more modest goal: cutting imports from Middle Eastern countries by 75 percent. That was less deceptive than speaking of "independence," but deceptive nonetheless. Only about one barrel of imported oil in every five was coming from the Middle East, so cutting that by 75 percent sounded like a bigger step than it really was. The biggest suppliers to the United States actually were Canada and Mexico.

In his speech to Congress, Bush proposed a mere 22 percent increase in government spending for clean-energy research, called "shockingly small" by Severin Borenstein, an energy economist at the University of California–Berkeley. This expert added that Bush's plan was "hardly the Manhattan Project equivalent on energy that we need."

It comes as no surprise that candidates want to avoid discussing politically painful solutions during an election year, or ever. But there's real harm in pretending that there are easy solutions to big problems, or that the problems don't exist. Accepting the spin means letting the problems fester; meanwhile, the solutions become even more painful, or the problems overwhelm us entirely.

The Profits of Disinformation

Deception is highly profitable. Consider the case of one California huckster calling himself "Dr." Alex Guerrero. He appeared on TV infomercials claiming that his "natural" herbal remedy Supreme Greens (containing grapefruit pectin) could cure or prevent cancer, arthritis, osteoporosis, fibromyalgia, heart disease, diabetes, heartburn, fatigue, or even "the everyday ravages of aging," all while promoting weight loss of up to four pounds per week and up to eighty pounds in eight months. A one-month supply cost $49.99, plus shipping and handling. And as incredible as "Dr." Guerrero's claims might seem, he sold enough Supreme Greens to drive around in a Cadillac Escalade. When the Federal Trade Commission hauled him into court he agreed to settle the case by halting his claims and either paying a $65,000 fine or giving the government title to his flashy SUV. And he was just one small-timer in the FTC's bulging case files.

According to the FTC, "consumers may be spending billions of dollars a year on unproven, fraudulently marketed, often useless health-related products, devices and treatments." Worthless weight-loss products alone have proliferated so wildly that in 2004 the FTC launched "Operation Big Fat Lie" to target them. As of October 2005, the commission said it had secured court orders requiring more than $188 million in consumer redress judgments against defendants. And since the FTC relies mostly on negotiated settlements, which are like plea bargains, that $188 million is most likely a fraction of the actual ill-gotten gains from weight-loss scams.

Deception Can Be Bad for Your Health

Deception is practically built into the business plans of some major corporations, and entire brands have been built on false advertising. Consider the long and checkered history of Listerine, for example. In 1923 the Lambert Pharmacal Company started marketing what had been a relatively ineffective hospital antiseptic as a mouthwash that could cure "halitosis," a medical term not much used until Lambert's ads made it a household word. Sales of Listerine exploded, going from $100,000 a year in 1921 to more than $4 million in 1927 and $7 million in 1930. But the ads were false: no mouthwash can cure bad breath. Bad breath has a variety of causes, including certain foods, smoking, gum disease, dry mouth, diabetes, and even dieting, which can't be offset by any mouthwash. As the American Dental Association now emphasizes in bold print on its website: "Mouthwashes are generally cosmetic and do not have a long-lasting effect on bad breath."

Other Listerine ads in the 1930s and 1940s claimed that the same product could cure "infectious dandruff" when rubbed on the scalp, a preposterous claim given that dandruff isn't caused by infection. For decades Listerine also claimed to cure sore throats and to reduce the likelihood of catching colds. As far back as 1931, *The Journal of the American Medical Association* railed against such false claims, saying "by its very name Listerine debases the fame of the great scientific investigator [Joseph Lister] who first established the idea of antisepsis." And yet Listerine kept right on making its claims, decade after decade, stopping in 1977 only after it lost a five-year legal battle with the Federal Trade Commission that went all the way to the U.S. Supreme Court. In a landmark case, the court upheld the commission's order to run a year's worth of corrective advertising, at a cost of $10.2 million, telling audiences that "Listerine will not prevent colds or sore throats or lessen their severity."

And still the spin continues. Listerine ads still imply the product cures offensive breath odor by saying it "kills the germs that cause bad breath." That's true but misleading. The germs come right back, as they always have. Lately, research has finally turned up a legitimate use for Listerine: it does slow the formation of dental plaque. But old habits die hard: Listerine (now owned by Pfizer) overstated its one virtue in a 2004 TV ad that claimed "Listerine's as effective as floss at fighting plaque and gingivitis. Clinical studies prove it." But the clinical studies proved no such thing, because they failed to ensure that the subjects using floss were using it correctly. A leading maker of dental floss sued Pfizer, and Judge Denny Chin of the U.S. District Court of Manhattan ruled that Pfizer's studies "proved only that Listerine is 'as effective as improperly-used floss.'" On January 6, 2005, he ordered the ads off the air. Chin also said the ads might be causing real physical harm: "I find that Pfizer's false and misleading advertising also poses a public health risk, as the advertisements present a danger of undermining the efforts of dental professionals . . . to convince consumers to floss on a daily basis." We'll have more to say about Listerine later, showing you how its advertising displayed classic warning signs of deception.

In extreme cases, commercial deception can cost lives. In May 2004, the FTC sued a Canadian outfit called Seville Marketing, Ltd., accusing it of deceptively advertising something called Discreet, supposedly a home test for HIV. Seville claimed its product was 99.4 percent accurate, but the U.S. Centers for Disease

Control and Prevention found that 59.3 percent of tested kits provided inaccurate results. These included both false HIV-positive results and false HIV-negative results. Buyers of Discreet would have done better by flipping a coin to see if they were infected or not.

It wasn't until a year later, May 18, 2005, that Seville agreed to settle the case, with a court order prohibiting the company from selling its test kits or making deceptive claims. Seville also agreed to let the FTC tell its customers that the product didn't work as advertised and that they should contact a health professional. The FTC offered no estimate of how many HIV-infected persons might have been lulled into a false sense of security by an erroneous negative reading. It is hard to avoid the conclusion that many people delayed treatment or unknowingly spread the virus to others because they were deceived by Seville's advertising.

Prescription-Strength Political Bunk

Politicians deliver even bigger doses of prescription-strength deception, deliberately filling voters' heads with disinformation about their opponents and about their own policies. One example is what we at FactCheck.org called a tax fable when it first surfaced in the 2004 campaign. The Republican National Committee chairman, Ed Gillespie, claimed in a speech on December 3, 2003, that under Bush's tax-cut bills "80 percent of the tax relief for upper-income filers goes to small businesses." It turned out that Gillespie's definition of "small" businesses actually included all partnerships, a category that includes the nation's biggest accounting firms, law firms, and real-estate partnerships, and "businesses" that are really only sidelines, such as occasional rental income from a corporate chief's ski condo. Gillespie was trying to support the argument that cutting federal income taxes for high-income individuals translates at least in part to a tax cut for small businesses, stimulating hiring and thus helping some lower-income workers, too. But Gillespie was counting every rich person who got even a dollar in income from a small business as a "small-business owner"—and counting every dollar of tax benefit they received as relief for small business. Under that preposterous definition President Bush and Vice President Dick Cheney both qualified as "small businesses," by virtue of $84 Bush received from an oil-drilling partnership, and the consulting income of Cheney's wife, Lynne. Neither "business" was a notable job producer.

The Bush campaign would use the same twisted reasoning in a TV ad against John Kerry, claiming that Kerry's proposal to scale back Bush's tax cuts for those making $200,000 a year or more would mean "900,000 small business owners would pay higher tax rates than most multinational corporations." In fact, according to analysis by the Tax Policy Center (a joint project of the Urban Institute and the Brookings Institution) the *maximum* number of small-business owners who could be affected—even by $1—was barely more than half the number the Bush ad claimed.

Voters Deceived

Not all voters are taken in by political snake oil, but many are. How many may surprise you. Bush's claim that Kerry's tax increase would have hit 900,000 small-business owners, for example, was found either "somewhat truthful" or "very truthful" by 62 percent of Americans polled after the 2004 election by the National Annenberg Election Survey. Only 24 percent found the statement "not too truthful" or "not truthful at all," and the rest didn't know or didn't answer. That means that of those who had an opinion, two and a half times as many had the wrong idea as had the right one.

The deception took in members of both parties, though of course not equally. Unsurprisingly, Republicans were more inclined to believe the Republican president's deception than were Democrats. Among Republicans, 76 percent found the claim truthful. But 64 percent of independents also found it truthful, and—

Dubious Campaign Claims Most Americans Believed

KERRY CLAIM: *The new jobs created since George W. Bush became president pay, on average, $9,000 a year less than the jobs they replaced.*

66%	Those finding statement "very truthful" or "somewhat truthful"

BUSH CLAIM: *John Kerry's tax plan would increase taxes on 900,000 small-business owners.*

62%	Those finding statement "very truthful" or "somewhat truthful"

Source: National Annenberg Election Survey, 2004. National telephone poll of adults Nov. 10–Dec. 15, 2004. Sample sizes: 1,669 for Kerry question, 1,731 for Bush question. The statistical margin of sampling error is +/- 2.4 percentage points.

what *is* surprising—nearly half of all Democrats did too. Forty-nine percent of them were inclined to believe Bush's unfounded claim that their own candidate would raise taxes on 900,000 small businesses.

Kerry deceived plenty of voters himself. Throughout the campaign he hammered away at the idea that the economy, which was finally creating hundreds of thousands of jobs after losing 2.6 million of them during Bush's first two and a half years in office, wasn't producing *good* jobs. Kerry insisted that the new jobs were paying thousands of dollars less than the old jobs that had disappeared, and he even claimed economists could measure the gap precisely. He said it in his acceptance speech to the Democratic National Convention and kept repeating it right through the third presidential debate, where he said, "The jobs the president is creating pay nine thousand dollars less than the jobs that we're losing."

That $9,000 figure was fanciful. It didn't actually compare the wages of lost jobs to those of newer jobs, because nobody gathers statistics in a way that allows such precise job-to-job comparisons. We know of no reputable economist who endorsed Kerry's figure, and quite a few who thought it was silly and misleading.

The existing evidence was mixed. One set of figures from the Bureau of Labor Statistics that grouped workers into different industries—manufacturing, for example, or health care—did suggest that job quality was declining. But that analysis was contradicted by a separate set of BLS figures, based on a different survey and grouping workers by occupation: doctor, nurse, assembly-line worker, engineer. The second set of figures suggested that job quality was improving. The Brookings Institution economist Barry Bosworth, a former Carter administration official, called Kerry's approach "very misleading," and added: "We shouldn't be in the business of trying to compare the rates of jobs lost to those gained because we just don't have the information right now to do it. Trying to measure the gross flow of jobs is really futile." And, we wish to add, deceptive.

Bogus as Kerry's claim was, two of every three persons polled after the election said they found it truthful. And that even included a majority of those who said they voted for Bush: 56 percent of them believed Kerry's baseless claim that new jobs paid $9,000 less than the old jobs.

Bush's Pack of . . . Wolves

Political deceivers don't always state their falsehoods outright; sometimes they merely imply them. But the effect can be just as bad. Our polling found that voters went to cast their ballots burdened by a severely distorted picture of both candidates, often because of deceptions subtly laid between the lines.

For example, one of the most deceptive ads of the 2004 campaign was a Bush commercial showing a pack of wolves, symbolizing terrorists about to attack. The announcer said Kerry had voted

Misleading TV Ad

PAID FOR BY BUSH-CHENEY 04, INC. AND THE REPUBLICAN
NATIONAL COMMITTEE AND APPROVED BY PRESIDENT BUSH.

Announcer: In an increasingly dangerous world—even after the first terrorist attack on America—John Kerry and the liberals in Congress voted to slash America's intelligence operations. By six billion dollars—cuts so deep they would have weakened America's defenses. And weakness attracts those who are waiting to do America harm.

(On screen: *several wolves eye the camera, as if preparing to attack.*)

Bush: I'm George W. Bush and I approve this message.

to cut intelligence spending "even after the first terrorist attack on America." We don't know whether that was intended to deceive, but it did. The "first attack" referred to was the truck bomb that went off in the parking garage under one of the World Trade Center towers more than a decade earlier—in 1993. But we spoke to many casual viewers who heard "first terrorist attack" and automatically thought of the first aircraft to hit the World Trade Cen-

ter on September 11, 2001, a terrifying event still vivid in voters'
memories.

The truth is that Kerry was supporting regular increases in
intelligence spending for several years prior to the attacks of September 11. But our postelection polling shows most citizens—
55 percent—found the statement that Kerry voted for intelligence
cuts after September 11 to be "truthful." That false notion may
have cost Kerry votes. And we believe the false picture of Kerry
foolishly trying to cut intelligence spending, even after a terrorist
attack that U.S. intelligence had failed to prevent, was encouraged
by the wording of Bush's ad and others like it.

The "Wolves" ad was deceptive in more direct ways as well. It
said Kerry voted to "slash" intelligence spending by $6 billion, "cuts
so deep they would have weakened America's defenses." In truth,
what Kerry supported was a $1 billion cut (as part of a much
broader deficit-reduction package), which would have continued
for five years. It amounted to a mere 3.7 percent of total intelligence spending. Would that have "weakened America's defenses"
as the ad claimed? In 1995, when he was a Republican congressman, Bush's own CIA director Porter Goss had proposed to cut
20 percent of the Central Intelligence Agency's staff. Kerry's dollar
cut didn't have to come from the personnel side of the ledger, so
Goss's Republican proposal would have cut more deeply into the
human resources of the CIA than Kerry's. But the Bush deception
worked. The public went to the polls with a mental picture of Kerry
as much weaker on intelligence spending than his actual record reflected. The Bush team hadn't lied, exactly. But they gave millions
of voters a false picture of Kerry's actual record on intelligence
spending.

Partisan Falsehoods Most Americans Believed

FALSEHOOD: *John Kerry voted for cuts in intelligence after September 11, 2001.*
Those finding statement "very truthful" or "somewhat truthful": 55 percent

FALSEHOOD: *The Bush administration permitted members of the bin Laden family to fly out of the United States while U.S. airspace was still closed after September 11, 2001.*
Those finding statement "very truthful" or "somewhat truthful": 52 percent

Source: National Annenberg Election Survey, 2004. Postelection telephone poll of adults, Nov. 10–Dec. 15, 2004. Sample size: 1,731 for both questions. The statistical margin of sampling error is +/–2.4 percentage points.

Bin Laden Baloney

Implied deception worked against Bush, too. Michael Moore's highly partisan movie *Fahrenheit 9/11* left many viewers, including the authors of this book, with the impression that President Bush had approved a special flight to allow relatives of Osama bin Laden who lived in the United States to get out of the country while U.S. airspace was still closed in the days immediately following 9/11. The movie also strongly implied that the bin Laden clan escaped without being questioned by U.S. officials about where Osama himself might be found, or about any prior knowledge of the attack. A close reading of Moore's script shows that Moore never stated that as a fact, but his implied message was unmistakable. Over newsreel footage of passengers stranded by the 9/11 grounding of all commercial flights, Moore is heard saying, "Who wanted to fly? No one. Except the bin Ladens." That is followed by footage of an airplane taking off, accompanied by the booming strains of The Animals' rock song "We Gotta Get Out of This Place." Then Moore says, "It turns out that the White House approved planes to pick up the bin Ladens." But as the final report of the independent 9/11 Commission later documented—possibly to clarify the widely held misimpression Moore had created—the flight carrying the bin

Laden relatives didn't depart until a full week after airspace was re-opened to commercial flights. Furthermore, the FBI questioned a number of the family members before they were allowed to leave.

Late in the campaign, Moore's sly insinuation was exceeded in mendacity by the Media Fund, an independent, Democratic-leaning group headed by former Bill Clinton deputy chief of staff Harold Ickes. It spent nearly $60 million in an attempt to defeat Bush. Part of that sum went to a radio ad saying that the bin Laden family had been allowed to fly "when most other air traffic was grounded." In fact, the bin Laden flight was on September 20, and the Federal Aviation Administration had allowed commercial air traffic to resume at eleven A.M. on September 13.

The radio ad also said, "We don't know whether Osama's family members would have told us where bin Laden was hiding. But thanks to the Bush White House, we'll never find out." That was utterly false. The FBI had questioned the family members—almost two dozen of them. Here's some of what the 9/11 Commission's final report said on that point:

> Twenty-two of the 26 people on the Bin Ladin flight were interviewed by the FBI. Many were asked detailed questions. None of the passengers stated that they had any recent contact with Usama Bin Ladin or knew anything about terrorist activity [pp. 557–58].

False Radio Ad

MEDIA FUND: "Flight Home"

Announcer: After nearly 3,000 Americans were killed, while our nation was mourning the dead and the wounded, the Saudi royal family was making a special request of the Bush White House. As a result, nearly two dozen of Osama bin Laden's family members were rounded up—not to be arrested or detained, but to be taken to an airport, where a chartered jet was waiting . . . to return them to their country. They could have helped us find Osama bin Laden. Instead the Bush White House had Osama's family flown home, on a private jet, in the dead of night, when most other air traffic was grounded.

We don't know whether Osama's family members would have told us where bin Laden was hiding. But thanks to the Bush White House, we'll never find out.

Furthermore, the 9/11 Commission said that the bin Laden family members might not have been interviewed had they simply departed the country in the usual way, rather than leaving on a charter flight with special White House clearance:

> Having an opportunity to check the Saudis was useful to the FBI. This was because the U.S. government did not, and does not, routinely run checks on foreigners who are leaving the United States. This procedure [chartering a flight] was convenient to the FBI, as the Saudis who wished to leave in this way would gather and present themselves for record checks and interviews, an opportunity that would not be available if they simply left on regularly scheduled commercial flights [p. 557].

Fifty-two percent of the people we polled found it truthful that the Bush administration let the bin Laden family leave the United States while airspace was still closed. In this case it was mostly Democrats who were deceived (perhaps because they wanted to be; more on that later): 70 percent of them found the false statement truthful. But nearly half the independents were taken in, too: 48 percent found it truthful. And more than one third of Republicans—36 percent—also bought the myth that Bush let the bin Laden clan skedaddle when airports were still closed.

Nonstop Deception

Political deception doesn't stop when elections are over. Even in nonelection years, interest groups now weigh in on legislative and other policy debates with TV ad campaigns on which they spend tens of millions of dollars. In 2005:

- In a radio ad by a conservative group called FreedomWorks, former Republican House leader Dick Armey misleadingly claimed a proposed reform of asbestos litigation set aside "billions of . . . tax dollars as payoffs to trial lawyers." In fact, trial lawyers had opposed the measure; it would have cut into their legal fees.

- A liberal group called Campaign for America's Future ran a grossly misleading newspaper ad claiming that Wall Street stockbrokers stood to get a $279 billion windfall from the individual Social Security accounts that Bush outlined in some detail in 2005. FactCheck.org dug up evidence that brokers could expect less than two pennies—yes, pennies—for every $1,000 invested.

- A conservative group called Let Freedom Ring, Inc., ran a pair of TV ads pushing for a $4 billion security fence along the Mexican border. The ad showed footage of the 9/11 attack on the World Trade Center with a voice-over claiming "illegal immigration from Mexico provides easy cover for terrorists." But none of the 9/11 hijackers entered the United States through Mexico, and all entered legally. More persons from suspect Muslim nations actually slip in over the Canadian border than from Mexico.

No Respect

As we hope is becoming clear, respect for facts isn't a major concern in the advertising industry, and is far too rare in politics.

"Surely it is asking too much to expect the advertiser to describe the shortcomings of his product," wrote David Ogilvy in his *Confessions of an Advertising Man.* The legendary adman said he was "continuously guilty of suppressio veri." That translates from the Latin as "suppression of truth," and it sums up a lot of what we see in commercial advertising. The art of advertising, in fact, has been described as the art of promoting a false illusion. "I've never worked on a product that was better than another. They hardly don't exist," the advertising executive George Lois told CBS News's

60 Minutes in 1981. "So what I have to do is, I have to create an imagery about that product."

The historian Doris Kearns Goodwin gives a good example of the attitude we are talking about in her 1991 book *Lyndon Johnson and the American Dream.* She reports that LBJ sometimes claimed that his great-great-grandfather had died at the Alamo, and at other times said he died at the Battle of San Jacinto, in which Sam Houston routed the Mexican dictator Antonio López de Santa Anna and won independence for Texas. The latter claim was particularly unlikely, since Houston lost only nine men killed in the twenty-minute battle. And, obviously, both claims could not be true. In fact, Goodwin learned that the great-great-grandfather to whom Johnson referred actually "died at home, in bed." When she challenged LBJ he said, "God damn it, why must all those journalists be such sticklers for details?"

Goodwin explains that Johnson was engaging in the old Texas tradition of the "tall tale." She quotes a literary historian, Marcus Cunliffe, who wrote that as the "tall tale" spread west it entered political oratory during an era when politics was among the few sources of entertainment: "Was it true? The question had little meaning. What mattered was the story itself."

The same notion surfaced again in 2006 when the author James Frey was exposed as having fabricated portions of his supposedly truthful memoir *A Million Little Pieces.* Oprah Winfrey, who had promoted the best-selling book to her devoted audience, at first defended the "underlying message of redemption" in the book, implying that it was acceptable to lie about the small stuff in the service of a laudable goal. But two weeks later she publicly apologized on her own show. "I left the impression that the truth does not matter," she said. "And I am deeply sorry about that, because that is not what I believe."

That's not what we believe either, and we'd like to see fewer tall tales and more respect for factual accuracy in politics, advertising, and public life in general. Count us among the "sticklers" who so irritated LBJ. The attitude we'd prefer was shown by the future Supreme Court Chief Justice John Roberts in 1986, when he was a young aide to President Ronald Reagan. Somebody had drafted a joke for Reagan to drop into his annual economic message: "I just turned 75 today, [but that's] only 30 degrees Celsius." That was incorrect: 75 degrees Fahrenheit is only 23.9 degrees on the Celsius scale. Reporters for *The New York Times,* poring over Roberts White House memos during Roberts's confirmation battle in 2005, found that he had corrected the president's prepared remarks. When Reagan actually delivered them, he said: "I heard a reference to my age this morning. I've heard a lot of them recently. I did turn 75 today, but remember, that's only 24 Celsius."

Unprotected Public

How do the deceivers get away with it? Truth-in-advertising laws give some protection from false claims in *commercial* advertising, but a lot still get through. A false ad can run for many months before regulators get it off the air. And even then, advertisers have learned to weasel-word their commercials so that their claims are literally accurate but still misleading. We'll have more to say about that later in this book. As for politicians, they actually have a legal right to lie in their television and radio ads. There is no federal law requiring truth in political ads at all, and the few states that have attempted such laws have had them overturned or found them ineffective.

Some believe that politicians can be sued for defamation if they stray too far from the truth, and they think that provides some protection to voters. It doesn't. The courts move too slowly for that, and they rightly give candidates the full benefit of the free-speech protections of the U.S. Constitution. So lawsuits for false political claims are rare, and do voters no good. In a classic case from the past, during the 1964 presidential election Barry Goldwater, the Republican candidate, sued *FACT* magazine for claiming he had a severely paranoid personality and was psychologically unfit for the high office. Goldwater won the lawsuit, but the verdict came down long after he had lost the election to Lyndon Johnson in a landslide. So for any who voted against Goldwater because they believed the magazine, the courts were no help. The attitude of the courts is that voters are grown-ups who deserve to hear all sides of an argument, even the falsehoods, and that it's up to them to sort it out for themselves.

Citizens might expect to find political spin aggressively debunked by the news media, but in our view they get far too little of that. There was a brief flurry of "factcheck"-style reports in the final weeks of the 2004 presidential campaign, but that was a departure from the norm. The fact that some news organizations were actually calling dubious claims "false" or "misleading" was itself considered newsworthy. The PBS *NewsHour* devoted a segment to the phenomenon on its evening newscast. Alas, the media fact-checking quickly faded once the election was over. The hard reality is that the public is exposed to enormous amounts of deception that go unchallenged by government regulators, the courts, or the news media. We voters and consumers must pretty much fend for ourselves if we know what's good for us. In coming chapters, we'll show you how.

Chapter 2

A Bridesmaid's Bad Breath

Warning Signs of Trickery

POOR EDNA. SHE WAS ONE GREAT-LOOKING WOMAN, SO IT WAS strange that she couldn't land a husband. And nobody would tell her why she was "often a bridesmaid but never a bride." Edna wasn't real, but her story, part of the ad campaign begun in 1923 that made Listerine lucrative, offers a window into how we can be manipulated by appeals to our fears and insecurities.

The reason Edna was headed for spinsterhood—according to the ads—was breath so offensive that "even your best friends won't tell you." The ploy worked: Lambert sold tanker loads of Listerine. In 1999, *Advertising Age* magazine named the "bridesmaid" ad one of the hundred top campaigns of the twentieth century.

The Listerine ads appealed to fear with a simple, unspoken message: use our product, or risk losing friends or even a future spouse because of putrid breath that you may not even know you have. Other Listerine ads played variations on the theme. In an ad from 1930, a dentist wonders why his patients have deserted him; he had never heard the whispers about his awful breath. The headline: "Do they say it of you?—*probably*." Another ad, from 1946, shows a young man rejected at a job interview and asks, "In these days of fierce competition to get and hold a job, can you afford to take chances because of halitosis (unpleasant breath)?"

WARNING SIGN: *If It's Scary, Be Wary*

FEAR HAS BEEN A STAPLE TACTIC OF ADVERTISERS AND POLITICIANS for so long that you'd think that we would have become better at detecting their use of it. But fear and insecurity can still cloud our judgment. To put the lesson in a nutshell: "If it's scary, be wary."

The FUD Factor

Fear sells things other than mouthwash. In the 1970s, one of IBM's most talented computer designers left to make and market a new machine. Gene Amdahl's "Amdahl 470" mainframe computer was a direct replacement for IBM's System 370, then the market leader, but sales were less than expected. Amdahl found that many corporate customers were afraid to buy his product even though by all accounts it was cheaper, faster, and more reliable than the IBM machine. He accused his former employer of using "FUD"—his acronym, meaning "fear, uncertainty, and doubt"—to discourage consumers from his new brand. Would Amdahl's company be around to support their hot new product? Would IBM retaliate somehow? Would corporate purchasers be fired for taking a risk if things went bad?

We see FUD being employed to sell all sorts of things. There are few Internet users who haven't run into frightening pop-up messages along the lines of this hit from 2004–05: "WARNING: POSSIBLE SPYWARE DETECTED . . . Spyware can steal information from your computer, SPAM your e-mail account or even CRASH YOUR COMPUTER!" Frightened recipients who clicked a link to "complete the scan" were taken to a website peddling a $39.95 product called SpyKiller, which promised to remove "all traces" of the fearsome spyware. But the Federal Trade Commission found this FUD-based pitch to be a lie. No scan had been performed before the message was sent, no spyware had been found, and the program didn't even work as advertised—it failed to remove "significant amounts" of spyware. In May 2005, the FTC took the Houston-based marketer, Trustsoft, Inc., to court, and the company and its chief executive, Danilo Ladendorf, later agreed to pay $1.9 million to settle the case. Ladendorf was to sell his Houston residence to pay back what the FTC called "ill-gotten gains," but by then tens of thousands of consumers had been tricked.

Bush's "Day of Horror"

The buildup to the 2003 invasion of Iraq showed a particularly able use of FUD. In his State of the Union address of January 28, 2003, President Bush said that Saddam Hussein was pursuing weapons of mass destruction and invited listeners to imagine what would have happened if Saddam had given any to the 9/11 hijackers: "It would take one vial, one canister, one crate slipped into this country to bring a day of horror like none we have ever known." The previous September, Condoleezza Rice, who was then the national security adviser, had said on CNN that it wasn't clear how quickly Saddam could obtain a nuclear weapon, then added: "But we don't want the smoking gun to be a mushroom cloud." With memories of September 11, 2001, still fresh, those appeals to fear helped generate overwhelming public support for the war. On March 17, 2003, three days before the war began, only 27 percent of those polled for

The Washington Post said they opposed the war. A lopsided majority of 71 percent said they supported it, including 54 percent who said they supported it "strongly."

Afterward, as we all know now, U.S. inspectors searched for months only to conclude that Saddam had actually destroyed his stockpiles of chemical and biological weapons years earlier. He had no active program to develop nuclear weapons. Bush's "day of horror" speech was as scary as scary gets. And many of us—the president, the CIA, Congress, and much of the press and the public—should have been more wary, should have asked more questions, and should have demanded more evidence.

Some circumstances justify raising an alarm: it's appropriate to shout "Fire!" when flames really put lives or property in immediate danger. Our point here is that a raw appeal to fear is often used to cover a lack of evidence that a real threat exists, and should alert us to take a hard look at the facts. Are we being warned, or deceived?

WARNING SIGN: *A Story That's "Too Good"*

WE SHOULD APPROACH CLAIMS CAUTIOUSLY WHEN THEY ARE TOO dramatic, especially when we want them to be true. Consider a case involving what we might call "destruction of mass weapons."

The book *Arming America: The Origins of a National Gun Culture* was greeted with celebration by advocates of gun control. The author, Michael A. Bellesiles, a professor of history at Atlanta's Emory University, claimed that household gun ownership had been rare in colonial and pre–Civil War America. Michael Barnes, the then president of Handgun Control, Inc. (now known as the Brady Campaign to Prevent Gun Violence), lauded Bellesiles's "discovery" and proclaimed: "By exposing the truth about gun ownership in early America, Michael Bellesiles has removed one more weapon in the gun lobby's arsenal of fallacies against common-sense gun laws."

If, indeed, weapons ownership wasn't widespread in colonial America, then the picture of a nation of "Minutemen" with muskets over the fireplace was false. This also meant the National Rifle Association would have less room to argue that the Second Amendment was written to guarantee the right of individuals to own guns privately, and not just to bear arms as members of a regulated militia. Bellesiles offered as proof what he described as a painstaking, ten-year study of 11,000 probate records showing what people owned when they died. Columbia University seemingly endorsed the finding, awarding Bellesiles's book the coveted Bancroft Prize in 2001.

For those favoring gun control, Bellesiles told a story that was way too good to be true—literally. "The data fit together almost too neatly," noted Professor James Lindgren of the Northwestern University School of Law. After checking a portion of the same records on which Bellesiles said he had based his conclusions, Lindgren and his colleagues concluded that he had "repeatedly counted women as men, counted guns in about a hundred wills that never existed, and claimed that the inventories evaluated more than half of the guns as old or broken when fewer than 10% were so listed." In eight different sets of probate records, guns appeared in 50 percent to 73 percent of estates left by men, figures several times higher than Bellesiles had claimed. Lindgren found guns were twice as common as Bibles in estates from 1774.

Other discrepancies were noted; for example, Bellesiles claimed to have examined probate records from San Francisco, but all such records had been destroyed in the 1906 earthquake and fire. Emory University placed Bellesiles on paid leave and asked a panel of outside historians to investigate. The investigators found "evidence of falsification" regarding the "vital" table summarizing Bellesiles's probate data and said "his scholarly integrity is seriously in question." He resigned from Emory, still protesting that he was guilty of nothing worse than innocent mistakes. Nevertheless, in December 2002 Columbia University withdrew the Bancroft Prize, saying that Bellesiles had "violated basic norms of acceptable scholarly conduct."

There was plenty of reason to question Bellesiles's data. Given how starkly it contradicted what had been accepted for two centuries, it amounted to an extraordinary claim demanding extraordinary proof. Gun-control advocates were too quick to swallow it because it seemed to help their cause, and they paid the price in embarrassment when the facts of Bellesiles's deception were uncovered. When a claim seems "too good," it should be a warning to withhold judgment until we get a close look at the evidence.

Data in the Service of Ideology

Extravagant claims are just too easy to accept when they match biases. In 1991, we were told something shocking, which seemed to confirm the view that women are victims of a sexist society. In her book *The Beauty Myth,* Naomi Wolf claimed that 150,000 women die annually from anorexia nervosa. This was a preposterously high number, more than five times the number of Americans who died of AIDS that year, for example. But it strongly supported Wolf's thesis that women were suffering because of an impossible standard of beauty imposed by society.

The 150,000 figure was disputed in 1994 by Christina Hoff Sommers, a critic of the feminist movement, who said "the correct figure is less than 100." While Sommers should be credited for debunking Wolf's wildly inaccurate claim, she, too, was way off, according to Harold Goldstein and Harry Gwirtsman of the Eating Disorders Program of the National Institute of Mental Health. They noted that between one half percent and one percent of the 28 million women between 15 and 29 years old were thought to have anorexia, and that a mortality rate of about 10 percent over a 20-year period was "generally accepted." That would work out to roughly 1,000 deaths per year, Goldstein and Gwirtsman figured. They also cautioned against accepting "data in the service of ideology." That's a notion we endorse. When the data square too nicely with your biases, always ask, "Is this dramatic story really true? Am I buying this just because I want it to be true? What's the evidence?"

WARNING SIGN: *The Dangling Comparative*

"LARGER," "BETTER," "FASTER," "BETTER-TASTING." ADVERTISERS FRE-quently employ such terms in an effort to make their product stand out from the crowd. In a recent ad, makers of New Ban Intensely Fresh Formula deodorant claimed it "keeps you fresher longer." One might be forgiven for thinking they meant it keeps you fresher, longer than the competition. But, as a competitor complained to the Better Business Bureau's National Advertising Division, they meant fresher than Ban's old formulation.

Politicians are particularly able users of this technique. In the 2004 presidential campaign, George W. Bush's TV ads hammered away with this line: "[John] Kerry supported higher taxes over 350 times." A voter might quite reasonably have thought this to mean that Kerry had voted to raise taxes an alarming number of times, but that implication was grossly misleading. Bush did not mean that Kerry had in every case voted to make taxes "higher" than they were at the time. Such votes were relatively rare. Employing a common political tactic, Bush counted every vote Kerry had cast *against a proposed tax cut,* which meant voting to leave taxes unchanged. He also padded the count by including many procedural votes on the same bills. Bush even counted some of Kerry's votes for Democratic tax cuts, reasoning that those would still leave taxes higher than the Republican alternatives. Thus, by means of twisted use of the dangling comparative, a vote for cutting taxes became a vote for "higher taxes."

Bush was using the phrase "higher taxes" without answering the question "Higher than what?" A dangling comparative occurs when any term meant to compare two things—a word such as "higher," "better," "faster," "more"—is left dangling without stating what's being compared. Bush used a dangling comparative to mischaracterize Kerry's actual record. Kerry did vote for several tax increases during his twenty years in the Senate, but nothing remotely close to 350. His voting record was consistent with his promise to repeal only part of Bush's tax cuts and to raise taxes only on persons earning more than $200,000 a year.

Please Mom, More Arsenic!

Just to be fair, we should note that the Democrats have been known to employ the dangling comparative with some skill themselves. In 2001, for example, President Bush was accused of trying to put "more arsenic" in drinking water. In April of that year, the Democratic National Committee ran a TV ad in which a little girl asks, "May I please have some more arsenic in my water, Mommy?" And at the January 4, 2004, debate among Democratic presidential hopefuls in Des Moines, Iowa, Representative Dick Gephardt of Missouri said the Bush administration "tried to put more arsenic in the water. We stopped them from doing it."

But by "more arsenic" Democrats did not mean "more than is in the water now"; the disagreement was over how much to *reduce* arsenic levels. When Bush took office he suspended a regulation that President Clinton had proposed only days before the end of his term. This last-minute regulation would have reduced the federal ceiling on arsenic in drinking water from 50 parts per billion (ppb), where it had been since 1942, to 10 ppb. The Bush administration said it wanted to review the costs being imposed on small communities, estimated to be as high as $327 per household for some towns of fewer than 10,000 people. Bush administration officials considered a more flexible limit that would have allowed a limit of as high as 20 ppb in a few cases. That would have been double the limit proposed by Clinton but still a 60 percent reduction compared to the existing ceiling. Eventually, however, Bush accepted the 10 ppb level and the new limit went into effect in January 2006 exactly as Clinton had proposed—no earlier, no later. At no time did the Bush team propose to raise the limit above the existing level to allow "more arsenic."

In both cases, the deceivers' central point may well have had a grain of merit, but rather than make an honest argument they invited the public to accept gross exaggerations. So when you hear a dangling comparative term such as "more" or "higher," always ask, "Compared to what?" The answer may surprise you—and keep you from being fooled.

WARNING SIGN: *The Superlatives Swindle*

JUST AS COMPARATIVE WORDS SUCH AS "MORE" AND "HIGHER" ARE warning signs, so are superlatives such as "most" and "highest" and claims such as "biggest in history" or "smallest ever." In 2004 a pro-Bush group named the Progress for America Voter Fund ran a TV ad asking, "Has any president been dealt a tougher hand?" Their message was that Bush, because he inherited an economy on the verge of a downturn and had presided during the terrorist attacks of September 11, 2001, faced the toughest circumstances of any president in history. That's silly. Was Bush "dealt a tougher hand" than Abraham Lincoln, whose election prompted the breakup of the Union and who took office just six weeks before Confederates fired on Fort Sumter and began the Civil War? Tougher than Franklin Roosevelt, who took office during the Great Depression and later contended with Japan's attack on Pearl Harbor in 1941? Come on!

Another example of the "superlative swindle": Republicans still persist in calling Bill Clinton's 1993 deficit reduction bill—in Bush's words—"the biggest tax increase in American history." It wasn't, unless you count only raw dollars and disregard population growth, rising incomes, a growing economy, and inflation. Measured as a fraction of the entire economy, Clinton's 1993 increase was one sixth the size of Roosevelt's 1942 tax increase. That World War II levy was equal to $5.04 for every $100 of economic output, according to a paper prepared by a tax expert in Bush's own Office of Tax Policy. Clinton's tax increase was equal to 83 cents.

Republicans have been victims of this tactic as well. The Sierra Club accused Bush of having the "worst environmental record in U.S. history." But "worst" by what measure? Even the Sierra Club admits that air got cleaner during Bush's tenure (nearly a 12 percent reduction in the six major pollutants between 2000 and 2005, according to official monitoring required by the Clean Air Act). And Bush—while certainly not as aggressive as the Sierra Club wanted— put in place much stricter controls on diesel emissions than had existed under his predecessor. In 2005, Bush also imposed the first federal controls on mercury emissions by power plants. We can't say who did have the "worst" record; but no president before Richard Nixon even had an Environmental Protection Agency, which was created in 1970.

Superlative claims can lead us to choose needlessly expensive products and make shallow political decisions. Approach them with care!

WARNING SIGN: *The "Pay You Tuesday" Con*

BY NOW NEARLY EVERYBODY WHO HAS INTERNET ACCESS IS PROBA-bly familiar with the Nigerian e-mail scams that have been going on since the 1980s. A supposedly wealthy or high-placed foreigner sends a message asking for financial help—today—to move millions of dollars out of his homeland, in return for a percentage of the money to be paid later. That this is a con should be obvious, but the U.S. Secret Service was still warning in 2006 that the Nigerian e-mail scam "grosses hundreds of millions of dollars annually and the losses are continuing to escalate."

The warning sign is simple: if it sounds like J. Wellington Wimpy, it's likely to be a trick. Wimpy, a friend of Popeye, was an unscrupulous glutton who tried to snag a free meal with the classic

© King Features Syndicate

line: "I will gladly pay you Tuesday for a hamburger today." That "pay you Tuesday" element should raise suspicions.

In politics it's a little different but the principle is the same. We, the voters, are going to get our hamburger today. That is, we will if only we vote for the right candidate, who promises we won't have to pay until Tuesday, if ever. The difference is that Wimpy doesn't intend to pay, but we or our children will have to. In general, Democrats promise social programs without mentioning future costs to taxpayers, while Republicans promise reduced taxes but are vague about future deficits or program cuts.

Democrats constantly promise to "preserve Social Security" without mentioning that to finance the benefits scheduled in current law will require a sizable tax increase. Official projections issued in May 2006 put the shortfall at $4.6 trillion over the next seventy-five years. To put that in perspective, the shortfall amounts to more than a third of the entire U.S. economy for the year 2006. To be paid Tuesday, of course.

Bush, for his part, promised to "pay Tuesday" for the war in Iraq, for his tax cuts, and for big increases in domestic spending, including a prescription drug benefit that is the largest expansion of Medicare in its history. The president assured the nation in his 2002 State of the Union address: "Our budget will run a deficit that will be small and short-term"—but as it turned out the deficit ballooned to $413 billion in 2004, a record measured in raw dollars and much above average even measured as a percentage of the economy. The deficit was still $318 billion the following year and an estimated $250 billion the next, and deficits of between $266 billion and $328 billion were projected each year for the remainder of the decade, according to the Congressional Budget Office. Those deficits are hardly "small" and certainly not "short-term," as the president had predicted. When "Tuesday" arrives somebody is going to be stuck with a very large tab.

WARNING SIGN: *The Blame Game*

To HEAR PRESIDENT BUSH TALK, YOU WOULD THINK THAT GREEDY lawyers are a major factor in the rising cost of health care. "One of the major cost drivers in the delivery of health care are [*sic*] these junk and frivolous lawsuits," he said in 2004. He insisted that doctors ordering needless tests and procedures for fear of being sued were costing federal taxpayers "at least $28 billion a year" in added costs to government medical programs. This claim rested mainly on a single 1996 study suggesting that "defensive medicine" accounted for 5 percent to 9 percent of total spending on health care. However, that conclusion had been contradicted by just about every other researcher who had looked at the problem.

The basis of Bush's blame-the-lawyers claim was disputed by both the Congressional Budget Office (CBO) and the Government Accountability Office (GAO), respected and politically neutral investigative agencies. After examining all the research on the subject, the CBO found "no evidence" that caps on damage awards of the sort Bush sought would reduce medical spending. "In short, the evidence available to date does not make a strong case that restricting malpractice liability would have a significant effect, either positive or negative, on economic efficiency," the CBO said.

Bush was engaging in the blame game, pointing a finger at an unpopular group and hoping to divert attention from the weakness of his own evidence. People who find their own position weak or indefensible often attack. That's why we say casting blame is a clue that the attacker may need a closer look than the person being blamed.

Blaming often occurs reflexively, out of pure partisanship and with little regard for facts. For example, a former Clinton aide, Sidney Blumenthal, suggested that George W. Bush was to blame for the flooding in New Orleans brought about by Hurricane Katrina in 2005. In a widely quoted article for Salon.com, Blumenthal wrote that "the damage wrought by the hurricane may not entirely be the result of an act of nature." He cited budget cuts by the Bush administration in flood-control projects in Louisiana. As later investigation revealed, however, the major cause of the flooding was the collapse of floodwalls and levees built before Bush took office. An engineering study commissioned by the National Science Foundation concluded that money was not the problem: "The performance of many of the levees and floodwalls could have been significantly improved, and some of the failures likely prevented, with relatively inexpensive modifications of the levee and floodwall system details." The report's author, Raymond Seed of the University of California–Berkeley, told reporters there was a "high likelihood" that human error was to blame, and possibly outright malfeasance: "Some of the sections may not have been constructed as they were designed." All this was underscored in June 2006 when the Army Corps of Engineers released a nine-volume study of the disaster, saying the New Orleans flood-control system failed to work as it was supposed to, and had so many weaknesses it had been "a system in name only." Whatever blame history will place on Bush's shoulders for his slow response to the flooding, Blumenthal was simply wrong to blame the president for the flooding itself.

Politicians' tendency to point fingers was epitomized by a T-shirt slogan we spotted: "When in doubt—blame liberals!" The word "conservatives" could fit just as well. Liberals like to blame "big oil companies" when gasoline prices shoot up, ignoring such factors as clean-air regulations that create local supply bottlenecks, or the surging global appetite for crude oil as China and other countries industrialize. Conservatives typically blame liberals for being "soft on crime," ignoring the steady rise in the U.S. prison population, to a point where as of mid-2005 nearly one in every 200 U.S. residents is serving time in a federal, state, or local lockup. And of course, whatever party is out of power always blames the incumbent president when the economy goes soft or the stock market tanks, even though the White House has only modest influence on global economic trends and markets.

When you hear people casting blame, take a close look at their facts. It's good to say to yourself, "That sounds like a one-sided case for the prosecution. What would the defense have to say about it?"

WARNING SIGN: *Glittering Generalities*

BEWARE OF ATTRACTIVE-SOUNDING BUT VAGUE TERMS — WHAT STUdents of propaganda techniques call glittering generalities. Coca-Cola isn't just carbonated water that's been flavored and sweetened, it's "the Real Thing." United isn't just an airline emerging from bankruptcy, it's your access to "the friendly skies." Allstate isn't just a colossal insurance company, it's "good hands." The U.S. Army isn't just a military organization, it's the "path of strength." The idea is to get you to buy the product without asking too many questions.

Perhaps the most popular glittering generality among politicians is that of mouthing support for the "middle class." In politics, it's hard to find a candidate who isn't for the middle class, because in America so few people think of themselves as lower-class or upper-class. In 2004, Democrat Dick Gephardt promised in his TV ads to "fight for America's middle class." John Edwards promised to "target tax cuts to the middle class." Howard Dean said he'd "strive for greater tax fairness for middle-class working families." Kerry said he "won't raise taxes on the middle class." And the president, not to be out-glittered, said "the middle class is paying less in federal taxes" because of his tax cuts.

Bush wasn't wrong: households earning between $40,000 and $50,000 in 2003 had received an average tax cut of $1,012, according to the nonpartisan Tax Policy Center. But richer families got a lot more. Households earning over $1 million saw cuts averaging $112,925. Kerry's definition of "middle class" included those earning as much as $200,000 a year: he promised not to raise taxes on anyone below that level. Dean and Gephardt, on the other hand, proposed to repeal all of Bush's tax cuts, including even those for people at the bottom of the federal income tax scale. So while all these politicians promised aid to the "middle class," their policies and definitions were quite different.

Learn to recognize glittering generalities, and you'll notice them flying at you from every direction. Lots of groups push for "affordable housing" but seldom define what that means in terms of price. A "right to privacy" sounds good, but should it prevent the FBI from asking who took out books on making explosives? Years ago, Vice President Dan Quayle frequently expressed support for "family values," but his support didn't extend to unwed mothers and their children. We learned that in 1992, when Quayle famously attacked the popular television sitcom character Murphy Brown, who had become a mother out of wedlock, for "mocking the importance of fathers by bearing a child alone and calling it just another lifestyle choice." Some other nice-sounding but vague terms to watch out for: dignity, honor, freedom, integrity, and justice (including both the "economic" and "social" varieties). It's always good to ask, "What do you mean by that, exactly?"

Chapter 3

"Tall" Coffees and
Assault Weapons

Tricks of the Deception Trade

ANYONE WHO HAS EVER STOPPED BY OUR MOST POPULAR COFFEE
chain knows that a "tall" coffee does not appear to be tall in relation
to anything else on the menu. Things are often not as they are described. "Large" olives are actually medium-sized. The Montana-
based Evergreen Foundation is supported by companies that cut
down trees, and the Washington-based Center for Consumer Freedom isn't run by consumers but was set up by a lobbyist for the
booze and tobacco businesses. And when a politician talks about a
"cut," he or she almost never means that spending will actually go
down.

Such deceptive tricks are so commonplace and obvious we can
shrug them off, ordering a "small coffee" or buying bottled olives
whose real size can be seen. But others deceive us when we let our
guard down. To remain unSpun, we need to recognize the common
tricks of the deception trade.

TRICK #1: *Misnomers*

THE SO-CALLED "ASSAULT WEAPON BAN" SIGNED BY PRESIDENT
Clinton in 1994 didn't really ban assault weapons—at least, not the
ones you see pictured so often in the hands of soldiers and terrorists. Fully automatic weapons of all kinds were outlawed around
the time of George "Machine Gun" Kelly and Bonnie and Clyde. It
has been illegal in the United States to own a real machine gun
since 1934 (except with an expensive and hard-to-obtain federal
permit). In fact, all that the assault weapon law "banned" was the
manufacture and import of certain *semiautomatic* weapons, which
can't be fired any faster than an ordinary pistol or rifle despite their
military-style looks. The very term "assault weapon ban" gave a misleading impression.

When Congress let the law expire in the midst of the 2004
presidential campaign, the misleading name was exploited for political benefit in a TV ad by the liberal political action committee
MoveOn PAC. "This is an assault weapon. It can fire up to three
hundred rounds a minute," the narrator said, while a fully automatic AK-47 appeared on screen. "In the hands of terrorists it could
kill hundreds." Those words were punctuated by the sound of a
rapid burst of machine-gun fire. "John Kerry, a sportsman and a
hunter, would keep them illegal."

Technically, those words were true: Kerry wasn't proposing to
repeal the 1934 law banning machine guns. But neither was Bush.
Nevertheless, MoveOn PAC's ad continued: "George Bush will let
the assault weapon ban expire. George Bush says he's making
America safer. Who does he think he's kidding?" The totality of
MoveOn's ad conveyed the utterly false message that Bush was
about to approve the sale of real, fully automatic assault weapons
that could "kill hundreds" in the hands of terrorists.

Much of the public was taken in by the ad. Language does our thinking for us, and people had been fooled in the first place by the statute's misleading name. After the election, the National Annenberg Election Survey asked respondents to evaluate the truthfulness of this statement: "The assault weapons ban outlawed automatic and semiautomatic weapons." The result: 57 percent found the statement to be either "very truthful" or "somewhat truthful," while only 28 percent said it was either "not too truthful" or "not truthful at all." By a margin of two to one, those who expressed an opinion had the wrong idea.

Even a simple term like "large" becomes misleading in the hands of the California Olive Industry. "California Ripe Olives grow in a variety of sizes: small, medium, large, extra large, jumbo, colossal and super colossal," the industry website informs us. Of the seven sizes, "large" is actually the third smallest. This sort of silliness seems to be escalating. The Starbucks Corporation doesn't even use the term "large." The smallest size on the menu is a "Tall" coffee (twelve ounces); the next size up is a "Grande" (sixteen ounces) and the largest size Starbucks calls "Venti" (twenty ounces).

Such puffery is so common that much of the time we aren't fooled, and can even make fun of it. When Seattle's Best coffee shops came up with a new name for their largest coffee, the humorist Dave Barry advised: "Listen, people: You should never, ever have to utter the words 'Grande Supremo' unless you are addressing a tribal warlord who is holding you captive and threatening to burn you at the stake. JUST SAY YOU WANT A LARGE COFFEE, PEOPLE." We think that's good advice.

Some names really can deceive, however, unless we keep our guard up. The makers of Smoke Away, a dietary supplement that purportedly helps people stop smoking in a week or less, paid $1.3 million in 2005 to settle a complaint by the Federal Trade Commission, which said there was no reasonable basis for the product's claim. Also in 2005 the FTC announced more than $1 million in settlements against marketers of dietary or herbal supplements misleadingly named Lung Support Formula (which supposedly cured asthma and emphysema), Antibetic Pancreas Tonic (claimed to cure diabetes), and Testerex (supposedly effective in treating 62 percent to 95 percent of cases of erectile dysfunction). The FTC called the claims "false and outrageous." In all those cases, the product names were mentioned as one factor contributing to the deception.

Don't assume that just because a law is called an assault weapon ban or a product is called Smoke Away that they really do what their names imply. Always ask, "What's behind that name? Does it really describe the thing they are trying to sell me? What would be a more accurate name for it?"

TRICK #2: *Frame It and Claim It*

FEW BUT THE RICH NEEDED TO THINK MUCH ABOUT THE FEDERAL estate tax, because it never touched the vast majority of Americans. In 1992, for example, the tax fell only on the richest 1.3 percent of those who died. But that's when a group backed by some billionaire families, including the Gallo wine clan and the Blethen family, owners of *The Seattle Times,* began lobbying to repeal it. They seemed to have so little chance that few paid any attention. But then somebody decided that rather than call the estate tax by its proper and legal name, activists should instead refer to it as the death tax. The man who claims credit for this is James L. Martin, head of the conservative 60 Plus Association. He tells of establishing a "beer and pizza fund" to which he required his employees to contribute $1 every time they slipped and uttered the term "estate tax." Other antitax crusaders picked up the name, and Republicans made it part of their political vocabulary around the time they took control of the House of Representatives in January 1995.

The term "death tax" was an intentional misnomer: obviously, what's being taxed isn't death, but bequeathed wealth. Nevertheless, the tactic worked. In 2001 the Republican-controlled Congress approved a gradual phase-down and temporary repeal, which will become permanent if foes of the tax get their way.

Why did this tactic work? The Republican strategist Frank Luntz explains. "The public wouldn't support it [repeal] because the word 'estate' sounds wealthy," he told an interviewer for the PBS documentary series *Frontline* in 2004. But call it a death tax, he added, "and suddenly something that isn't viable achieves the support of 75 percent of the American people. It's the same tax, but nobody really knows what an estate is. But they certainly know what it means to be taxed when you die."

Although the term "death tax" was misleading, it framed the issue in a way that made people think of the tax unfavorably even before they considered any facts. A simple rule of persuasion holds, "Frame the issue, *claim* the issue." Some supporters of the estate tax later regretted they had been so slow to frame the issue their way, as the "Paris Hilton tax cut." Indeed, in 2006 the Coalition for America's Priorities ran TV and radio ads calling estate tax repeal a giveaway to "billionaires and heiresses." The radio ad featured a Hilton imitator praising the Senate as "awesome" for considering repeal: "So what that gas is over three dollars a gallon? Like . . . use a credit card!" As we write this, Congress is still debating whether to repeal the tax permanently or just narrow it radically to a very few, very rich families. Either way, the "death tax" misnomer was a powerful weapon that the other side was slow to counter.

Democrats had better luck framing an issue when they attacked President Bush's Social Security plan. Bush proposed to create an option for younger workers to divert up to 4 percent of their wages through the payroll tax to personal accounts, which would be invested in government-approved mutual funds. Critics, among them the AFL-CIO, called this "Bush's plan to privatize Social Security," as though the entire Social Security program would somehow move from governmental control to private ownership, which wasn't at all what Bush was proposing. At a time when massive corporate fraud was being exposed at Enron and other major corporations, and the stock market had taken a huge dive, "privatizing" even part of one's retirement nest egg was a frightening idea; it implied taking the retirement program out of the hands of the government and turning it over to Wall Street speculators. In 2002, CNN correspondent John King asked the president about "your plan to partially privatize Social Security," and Bush protested: "We call them personal savings accounts, John."

Bush, of course, was trying to frame the issue his way; calling the accounts "personal savings" made it sound as though the owners would control their retirement money themselves, as they would a checking account. In fact, the accounts Bush eventually proposed allowed only a handful of investment choices, with little or no choice in how money could be paid out at retirement. Both sides used misleading words in the debate, but Bush's nomenclature didn't catch on. When he made a strong push for passage in 2005, opponents kept calling the plan "privatization," and the idea was quietly dropped for lack of support. The issue had not been framed as Bush wished, as one of potential gain for younger workers. It had been framed as one of potential loss for Social Security beneficiaries generally.

George Lakoff, a professor of linguistics at the University of California–Berkeley, has argued in a best-selling book, *Don't Think of an Elephant,* that conservatives have been far better than liberals at framing issues in this way. He says that President Bush successfully framed the tax debate by talking about "tax relief," as though taxes were an affliction, rather than "your membership dues in America," as Lakoff would prefer. He also cites Bush's use of terms such as "compassionate conservatism" and "No Child Left Behind" to make Republican policies more palatable to swing voters. "This is the use of Orwellian language—language that means the opposite of what it says—to appease people in the middle," he argues.

Lakoff's solution, however, is more such language—from the left. His Rockridge Institute is working on a "Handbook for Progressives" to assist his side. Even that title is instructive: note that the term "progressive" sets us up to think of people in favor of "progress," advancing toward a bright future. Had he called it a "Handbook for Liberals" he would have used a more neutral term— but one that has lost popularity.

For the ordinary citizen or voter, the important thing is to recognize that both sides try to use words that we'll automatically accept or reject without thinking too much. Indeed, sometimes just choosing a word means choosing sides. When discussing abortion, which word do you choose, "fetus" or "baby"? Are you "pro-choice" or "pro-life"? But there's generally much more to any issue than a name or a slogan can tell us. Judging an issue or a product by its name is as foolish as judging a book by its cover. Better to say to yourself, "Okay, that's what they want me to think. Now what's the rest of the story?"

TRICK #3: *Weasel Words*

ANYONE WHO HAS GONE TO A SALE AT A RETAIL STORE IS FAMILIAR with the principle of "weasel words." Weasel words suck the meaning out of a phrase or sentence, the way that weasels supposedly suck the contents out of an egg, leaving only a hollow shell. In "Up to 50 percent off," the empty shell of a phrase is "50 percent off," the weasel words are "up to." "Fifty percent off" means half price, period. Having added the words "Up to," the store can offer a single item at half price and mark down everything else by far smaller amounts, or not at all, and still, technically, be telling the truth.

Publishers Clearing House became the biggest magazine seller in America using lines such as "You May Already Be a Winner!" on the outside of their mailed sales pitches. "May" was the weasel word: the vast majority of recipients, of course, won nothing. In 2000, California and several other states sued PCH, accusing it of sending deceptive mailings labeled, for example, "[Consumer's Name]: WINNERS CONFIRMATION FORM ENCLOSED" or "PCH FINAL NOTIFICATION FOR TAX-FREE $11,700,000.00 SUPERPRIZE." That went beyond weasel wording to imply that the recipients *were* winners, according to the lawsuit. PCH denied any deception but agreed to refund $16 million to certain "high-activity" customers, and to make clear in future mailings that the consumer hadn't yet been determined to be a winner. Qualifying language was to be equal in prominence to "winner" language.

More weasel words: Hawaiian Punch "Fruit Juicy Red" is only 5 percent fruit juice, according to the manufacturer. The other 95 percent is nearly all sugar water and coloring. "Juicy" is the weasel word, meaning something less than "juice." Estée Lauder says its "Skin Perfecting Creme Firming Nourisher" makes "tiny lines seem to disappear." "Seem" is the weasel word in that pitch; the wrinkles, of course, don't really disappear. Egg Beaters advertise "the taste of real eggs," but the product is really only egg whites colored by beta carotene, plus other non-egg ingredients. To get a "taste of" something means you aren't getting it all.

Journalists are as guilty as anybody. Words such as "largely" conceal a writer's ignorance of the true number. "Largely" could mean anything up to half. "Most" means more than half, but how much more? "Several" can mean any number higher than two or three, but less than "many." A sentence that begins "Fifty-three Nobel Prize–winning scientists" has specific meaning, and the writer should be able to name all fifty-three if challenged. But a sentence that starts with "Many scientists" is a hollow shell that should alert us to the possibility that the writer is a bit hazy about the facts. One of the first things a journalist learns is how to "write around it" when a deadline is looming and there's no time to fill a factual hole in the story. Readers should be aware of the weasel words used to disguise those holes.

TRICK #4: *Eye Candy*

IF YOU JUST LISTENED TO THE ANNOUNCER, A TV AD FOR THE ANTI-depressant prescription drug Paxil CR was quite direct about some of the unpleasant consequences that might result from taking it: "Side effects may include nausea, sweating, sexual side effects, weakness, insomnia, or sleepiness." But if you just looked at the pictures on screen, you got a totally different impression. An attractive young woman was shown walking her dog in a park, chatting with friends, smiling, obviously depression free. She wasn't sweating or sick to her stomach. She was strong, not weak. Her eyelids weren't drooping, nor was she complaining of a sleepless night. The announcer continued: "Don't stop taking Paxil CR before talking to your doctor, since side effects may result from stopping the medicine." The announcer was in effect saying that this drug can even cause withdrawal symptoms for those who quit "cold turkey," but what viewers were seeing on screen were some laughing construction workers happily taking a coffee break from the job. Viewers weren't seeing any of the undesirable possible side effects they were being told about, and as a result, many of them probably weren't actually hearing the words or taking them into account.

Propagandists know that when words say one thing and pictures say another, it's the pictures that count. Scholars tell us that redundancy is correlated with retention. To minimize retention, a propagandist says one thing while showing the opposite. When the two differ, what we see tends to override what we hear.

Drug companies have become particularly adept at showing us smiling faces and flowery pictures while the narrator recites material they hope we won't notice, such as those lists of unpleasant and even debilitating or dangerous possible side effects. In this case, the FDA thought that GlaxoSmithKline, the makers of Paxil CR, had gone too far. On June 9, 2004, the FDA ordered the ad off the

air as "false or misleading," partly because it "fails clearly to com-
municate the major risks associated with Paxil CR." The FDA
denounced the use of pictures and sound to overwhelm the announcer's words. "The compelling and attention-grabbing visuals
and other competing modalities, such as background music . . .
make it difficult for consumers adequately to process and compre-
hend the risk information," the FDA said.

The CBS reporter Lesley Stahl learned about this same effect
the hard way. According to Stahl, she was worried that a report in
which she criticized Ronald Reagan during his 1984 reelection
campaign was so tough that her White House sources might
"freeze me out." No worries: a Reagan aide, Richard Darman,
called her afterward to say "What a great piece. We loved it." As
Stahl wrote in her book *Reporting Live,* the exchange continued:

> STAHL: "Why are you so happy? Didn't you hear what I said?"
> DARMAN: "Nobody heard what you said."
> STAHL: "Come again?"
> DARMAN: "You guys in Televisionland haven't figured it out, have
> you? When the pictures are powerful and emotional, they over-
> ride if not completely drown out the sound. Lesley, I mean it, no-
> body heard you."

Her TV story had shown generally upbeat pictures of Reagan,
and according to Darman those pictures were all that viewers carried away from her critical report. Darman had explained the basic
principle of the "eye candy" effect: pictures tend to overpower spoken words. It's just the way we human beings are wired.

Research by Kathleen Jamieson documented the eye candy
effect in 1988 and 1989. During the presidential election campaign of 1988, groups of voters were asked what they remembered
seeing in news in the past week. In one week, ABC News correspondent Richard Threlkeld had debunked distortions in both an
ad by Republican nominee George H. W. Bush and an ad by
Democratic nominee Michael Dukakis. To the surprise of the mod-

erators, some ABC viewers could recall what the ads said, but not what Threlkeld had said about them. In 1989, Jamieson showed audiences the full twenty-two minute newscasts that included the Threlkeld piece and then asked the viewers to write down everything they remembered from Threlkeld's report. Only thirty minutes after seeing the debunking, viewers still remembered the attacks in the Bush and Dukakis ads better than the reporter's corrections. The reason? Threlkeld had illustrated his stories by filling up the screen with the political spots, while his criticisms were spoken.

Just as Darman would have predicted, Threlkeld's spoken words were overwhelmed by the provocative pictures and graphics. In the Republican ad, printed text specifying weapons systems the Democrat supposedly opposed was superimposed over video of Dukakis riding in a tank. In the Democratic ad, a Social Security card was torn up. Viewers failed to get Threlkeld's message, which was that Dukakis actually favored some of the weapons the ad said he opposed and that the two candidates had the same position on Social Security.

These days TV reporters who do "adwatch" stories are usually careful to avoid the eye-candy effect. That's thanks in part to Annenberg's research. Annenberg advised reporters to use special graphic techniques, showing the offending ad "boxed" in a cartoon-like TV set so that viewers don't confuse the ad's message with the reporter's message, and imposing graphics over the ad to reinforce their points of criticism. But deceivers have learned a trick or two also, as we see in those pharmaceutical ads that use feel-good pictures to soften the unpleasant truth about the potential side effects of their products. Also, politicians have taken to slapping their slogans on banners and backdrops where TV cameras necessarily show them, so the speaker's message gets across visually even if the news soundtrack doesn't contain a single word he or she spoke.

An example of that is President Bush's appearance on November 30, 2005, at the U.S. Naval Academy. His message of the day—

A message conveyed by "eye candy." AP Images.

that he had a "plan for victory" in Iraq—was reinforced with banners above and below the podium. We can make fun of Bush for appearing in front of a banner reading "Mission Accomplished" two and a half years earlier, on May 1, 2003, aboard the aircraft carrier U.S.S. *Abraham Lincoln.* That bit of eye candy was, to say the least, premature. But, regardless of what the reporters were saying about them, each of Bush's messages was punched through by visuals that were powerful, whether or not they were valid.

Visuals also can be used to reinforce a false message that the deceiver can't state outright. In 2005 the abortion rights group NARAL Pro-Choice America ran a TV ad showing a bombed-out abortion clinic and a disfigured victim, while the voice-over said that Supreme Court nominee John Roberts "filed court briefs supporting violent fringe groups and a convicted clinic bomber," and adding: "America can't afford a justice whose ideology leads him to excuse violence." Roberts had in fact condemned clinic bombers and violence, but those powerful pictures transmitted the emotional message that Roberts had endorsed the mayhem being shown, even though the narrator stopped just short of saying that explicitly. FactCheck.org called that ad false and NARAL quickly pulled it off the air. Even the group's allies criticized it.

When you see dramatic images, listen to the "fine print." Ask yourself, "What are my *ears* telling me about this picture?" A picture can indeed be worth a thousand words—but those words aren't necessarily true.

TRICK #5: *The "Average" Bear*

SOMETIMES THE "AVERAGE" BEARS WATCHING. PRESIDENT BUSH sold his tax cuts to the public by claiming the "average tax cut" would be $1,586, but most of us were never going to see anywhere near that much. Half of Americans got $470 or less, according to the nonpartisan Tax Policy Center. Bush wasn't lying, just using a common mathematical trick. When most people hear the word "average" they think "typical." But the average isn't always typical, especially when it comes to the federal income tax: very wealthy people pay a very large share of the taxes and stand to get a very large share of benefits when those taxes are cut.

To see the "average bear" trick clearly, consider this simplified example. Imagine a small town of a thousand persons, including one superrich resident whom we'll call Gil Bates. Everybody in town is getting a tax cut this year: $10 for everybody but Mr. Bates, who is getting a whopping cut of $90,010. What's the average? Divide the sum of all the tax cuts ($100,000) by the total number of residents (1,000) and the *average* works out to $100 per resident. But that's not the *typical* cut. In our example, the average tax cut was ten times as large as the typical tax cut. Bush's "average" figure was like that. Big reductions for a relative few at the top of the income scale pulled up the average to a figure higher than was typical for most working Americans.

Bush also likes to point to increases in "average" income since he took office, as though everybody were enjoying improved financial well-being. For example, his White House staff issued a "fact sheet" in February 2006 that crowed, "Real after-tax income per person has risen 7.9 percent" since the president took office five years earlier. That figure accurately cites the latest quarterly statistics from the Department of Commerce, and it's true that many Americans did very well financially during Bush's first five years. But the average is misleading. Most of the gains were at the top, and many if not most Americans lost ground.

We know that was true for Bush's first four years, because for that period we have a better measure: a median figure, not an average. The median is the midpoint: half do better, half do worse. In 2005, according to a massive annual survey conducted by the Census Bureau, the median inflation-adjusted income per household since Bush took office had *fallen* by 2.7 percent, to $46,326. That's a before-tax figure, not strictly comparable to the after-tax figure the president prefers, but the $470 tax cut we mentioned earlier (also a median figure) wouldn't make up for the $1,273 decline in median before-tax income.

Other statistics fill in a picture of upper-income Americans gaining while lower-income Americans slipped back during this time. The strongest of these is the poverty rate, which went up under Bush, from 11.3 percent in Bill Clinton's final year to 12.6 percent in 2005. An estimated 5.4 million Americans fell into poverty, more people than live within the city limits of Chicago and Houston combined. This is a good example of why we say that the "average" bears watching.

When you hear "average," always ask, "Does that really mean 'typical'?" A single number seldom tells the whole story, especially with something as big and complicated as the U.S. economy or the federal tax system.

TRICK #6: *The Baseline Bluff*

THIS ONE IS A FAVORITE OF DEMOCRATS IN THE UNITED STATES, but it works in other countries as well. In Britain's 2005 elections, the Labour party plastered yellow "Warning" posters all over Britain claiming "The Tories will cut £35bn from public services." Actually, the Tories planned to *increase* spending, by £181 billion. But that increase was £35 billion smaller than the one Labour planned, so Labour called it a cut. As the British television network Channel 4 put it on their own "FactCheck" website: "In nominal terms, therefore, the £35bn is just a smaller increase, rather than a cut."

The same trick is used over and over in U.S. elections. In 1996, Bill Clinton accused his opponent, Bob Dole, of trying to "cut" Medicare by $270 billion. Actually, Dole and Republicans in Congress had never proposed to reduce the amount of money spent on Medicare, merely to hold down the rate of increase. Their plan could only be called a "cut" in relation to projected future spending, what budget experts like to call the "baseline." Clinton himself had proposed a "cut" of $124 billion in projected Medicare spending, without calling it that.

John Kerry used the same tactic late in his 2004 campaign, running an ad saying "Bush has a plan to cut Social Security benefits by 30 to 45 percent." That was simply false. Bush had stated repeatedly there would be no changes in benefits for anyone already getting them. What Kerry was referring to was a proposal, which Bush eventually embraced, to hold future benefit levels even with the rate of inflation, rather than allowing them to grow more quickly, in line with incomes. Over a very long period of time, that would mean benefit levels perhaps 45 percent lower than they would have been under current benefit formulas (assuming, for the sake of argument, that Congress enacted the tax increases necessary to finance those). But most of the future retirees who might ex-

perience that 45 percent "cut" were still unborn at the time Kerry
ran the ad.

When you hear a politician talking about a "cut" in a program
he or she favors, ask yourself, "A cut compared to *what*?"

TRICK #7: *The Literally True Falsehood*

SOMETIMES PEOPLE PICK WORDS THAT ARE DECEPTIVE WITHOUT
being strictly, technically false. President Clinton, who had an affair with one of his female interns, didn't object when his lawyer
told a judge that the intern had filed an affidavit saying "there is absolutely no sex of any kind in any manner, shape or form, with President Clinton." Clinton later said that statement was "absolutely"
true. How could he endorse the statement that "there is absolutely
no sex of any kind," given the shenanigans that actually went on? In
his grand jury testimony of August 17, 1998, Clinton offered this
famous explanation:

> PRESIDENT CLINTON: It depends on what the meaning of
> the word "is" is. . . . If "is" means is and never has been that is
> not—that is one thing. If it means there is none, that was a com-
> pletely true statement.

In other words, there had been sex, but not at the moment
when the statement was made in court. Clinton went too far: U.S.
District Judge Susan Webber Wright later found Clinton in civil
contempt for giving "intentionally false" testimony. (He also denied
having "sexual relations" with Lewinsky.) His license to practice
law in Arkansas was suspended for five years and he was fined
$25,000. He also gave up his right to appear as a lawyer before the
U.S. Supreme Court rather than face disbarment proceedings there.
But even though redefining "is" didn't work for Clinton, his remark

shows us how clever deceivers can try to mislead us without—in their minds, at least—actually lying.

"Reduced fat" may be a literally true claim, but it doesn't mean "low fat," just less fat than the product used to have. "Unsurpassed" doesn't mean "best"; it is just a claim that the product is as good as any other. "Nothing better" might also be stated as "as good but no better." And the claim that a product is "new and improved" doesn't signify that it is any good. What advertisers are trying to say is "Give us another try—we think we've got it right this time."

The Stouffer's Food Corp. made a literally true but misleading claim about its Lean Cuisine frozen entrées in 1991, in a $3 million advertising campaign that said: "Some things we skimp on: Calories. Fat. Sodium . . . always less than 1 gram of sodium per entrée." One gram of sodium is quite a lot. Dietary sodium is usually measured in milligrams—thousandths of a gram—and Lean Cuisine entrées contained about 850 milligrams. That's about a third of the FDA's recommended total intake for a full day, and too much to be called "low sodium" under public guidelines. The Federal Trade Commission ordered Stouffer's to stop making the claim. Whether or not it was literally true, the FTC concluded, "the ads were likely, through their words or images, to communicate a false low-sodium claim."

KFC Corporation used the same sort of "literally true falsehood" in an attempt to palm off fried chicken as health food. One of its ads showed a woman putting a bucket of KFC fried chicken down in front of her husband and saying, "Remember how we talked about eating better? Well, it starts today!" The narrator then said, "The secret's out: two Original Recipe chicken breasts have less fat than a BK Whopper."

That was literally true, but barely. The fried chicken breasts had 38 grams of total fat, just slightly less than the 43 grams in a Burger King Whopper. However, the chicken breasts also had three times more cholesterol (290 milligrams versus 85 milligrams), more than twice as much sodium (2,300 milligrams versus 980 milligrams), and slightly more calories (760 versus 710), according to the Federal Trade Commission. Not to mention that saying that something has less fat than a Whopper is like calling a plot of ground less polluted than your local landfill. The FTC charged KFC with false advertising, and KFC settled by agreeing to stop claiming that its fried chicken is better for health than a Burger King Whopper.

And of course, Clinton isn't the only politician to tell a literally true falsehood. In 1975, the former CIA director Richard Helms told reporters, "So far as I know, the CIA was never responsible for assassinating any foreign leader." That was true, but Helms didn't mention that the CIA had *attempted* assassinations of Fidel Castro and a few other foreign leaders. As the then CBS reporter Dan Schorr later noted, "It turned out as Helms said, that no foreign leader was directly killed by the CIA. But it wasn't for want of trying." Another example: In 1987 interviews, then Vice President George H. W. Bush told reporters that he was "out of the loop" about the arms-for-hostages trade known as Iran Contra. Most of us would interpret "out of the loop" as "Nobody told me." Bush once said in passing to CBS's Dan Rather that he had a different definition: "No operational role." A careful listener might have caught that Bush was denying only that he was running the operation, not denying that he knew of it or approved of it. Sure enough, years later a special prosecutor made public a diary entry by Caspar Weinberger, who was the U.S. secretary of defense at the time, saying that Bush was among those who approved a deal to gain release of five hostages being held by Iran in return for the sale of 4,000 wire-guided antitank missiles to Iran via Israel.

When you hear vague phrases or carefully worded claims, always ask, "Are they really saying what I think they're saying? What do those words mean, exactly? And what might they be leaving out?"

TRICK #8: *The Implied Falsehood*

WHEN THE UNITED STATES WENT TO WAR AGAINST IRAQ IN 2003, most Americans believed that Saddam Hussein had something to do with the terrorist attacks of September 11, 2001. And after the 2004 election, most Americans had the impression that President Bush had told them as much. The National Annenberg Election Survey's postelection poll found that 67 percent of adults found the following statement to be truthful: "George W. Bush said that Saddam Hussein was involved in the September 11 attacks." Only 27 percent found it untruthful.

In fact, Bush never said in public (or anywhere else that we know of) that Saddam was involved in the 9/11 attacks. The CIA didn't believe Saddam was involved, and no credible evidence has ever surfaced to support the idea. "We have never been able to prove that there was a connection there on 9/11," Vice President Dick Cheney said in a CNBC interview in June 2004. But he also said he still thought it possible that an Iraqi intelligence official had met lead hijacker Mohamed Atta in the Czech Republic in April 2001, despite a finding to the contrary by the independent 9/11 Commission. "We've never been able to confirm or to knock it down," Cheney said. To many ears, Cheney was saying he believed there *was* a connection, and that he lacked only the proof. In fact, after an exhaustive effort to confirm the meeting, U.S. intelligence agencies had found no credible evidence.

Advertisers often try to imply what they can't legally say. One marketer sold a product he called the Ab Force belt, which caused electrically stimulated muscle twitches around the belly. The Federal Trade Commission cracked down on similar products that overtly claimed that their electronic muscle stimulation devices would cause users to lose fat, reduce their belly size by inches, and create well-defined, "washboard" or "sixpack" abdominal muscles without exercising. In some of the most frequently aired infomercials on national cable channels in late 2001 and early 2002, sellers made claims including, "Now you can get rock hard abs with no sweat. . . . Lose 4 Inches in 30 Days Guaranteed. . . . 10 Minutes = 600 Sit-Ups." Launching what it called "Project AbSurd," the FTC got those blatantly false claims off TV and got the marketers to agree to pay $5 million. (They had sold $83 million worth of belts, the FTC said.)

But the Ab Force marketer persisted. He said his own advertising never made *specific* claims—which was true: it just showed images of well-muscled, bare-chested men and lean, shapely women, with close-ups of their trim waists and well-defined abdominals. And, of course, he had named his device Ab Force. The case went to a hearing at the FTC, where regulators presented some convincing evidence of how an unstated message can still get across. The Ab Force ads were shown to groups of consumers, 58 percent of whom later said the ads were telling them that the belt would cause users to lose inches around the waist, while 65 percent said they got the message that the product would give users well-defined abdominal muscles. The FTC's administrative law judge ruled that the unstated message implied by the ad, combined with the Ab Force name, constituted false advertising.

When the full commission voted unanimously to uphold the judge's order, it said the marketer had managed to sell $19 million of his belts even though his ads made no specific claim. "It illustrates how false and unsubstantiated claims can be communicated indirectly but with utter clarity—to the detriment of consumers and in violation of the laws this Commission enforces," the FTC's decision stated.

When you see or hear something being strongly implied but not stated outright, ask yourself, "Why do they have to lay it between the lines like that? Why don't they just come out and say it?" Often there's a very good reason: what the speaker wants you to believe isn't true.

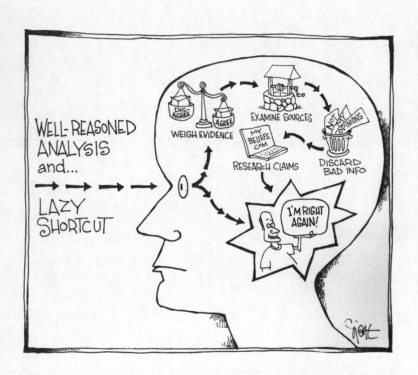

Chapter 4

UFO Cults and Us

Why We Get Spun

A man with a conviction is a hard man to change. Tell him you dis-
agree and he turns away. Show him facts or figures and he questions your sources. Appeal to logic and he fails to see your point.

—LEON FESTINGER, et al., *When Prophecy Fails* (1956)

HAVE YOU EVER WONDERED WHY OTHER PEOPLE ARE SO UNREASON-
able and hard to convince? Why is it that they disregard hard facts
that prove you're right and they're wrong? The fact is, we humans
aren't wired to think very rationally. That's been confirmed recently
by brain scans, but our irrational reaction to hard evidence has
been the subject of scholarly study for some time. Consider one of
the most famous scientific observations in all of psychology, the
story of a UFO cult that was infiltrated by the social psychologist
Leon Festinger and his colleagues half a century ago.

They observed a small group of true believers whose leader was a woman the authors called Marian Keech, in a place they called Lake City. Mrs. Keech said she had received messages from beings called Guardians on Planet Clarion saying that North America would be destroyed by a flood, but that her followers would be taken to safety on a UFO a few hours earlier, at midnight on December 21, 1954. Members of her cult quit jobs, sold possessions, dropped out of school, and prepared for the space journey by removing metal objects from their clothing as instructed by Mrs. Keech. They gathered in her living room on the appointed night, and waited.

Midnight came and went, and of course neither the flood nor the promised spacecraft arrived. But did the faithful look at this incontrovertible evidence and conclude, "Oh, well, we were wrong?" Not a chance. At 4:45 A.M., as morning approached, Mrs. Keech told them that she had received another message: the cataclysm had been called off because of the believers' devotion. "Not since the beginning of time upon this Earth," she said, "has there been such a force of Good and light as now floods this room." And then she told the group to go spread the word of this miracle. One member walked out, fed up with Keech's failed predictions, but the others were jubilant. In the days that followed, Festinger and his colleagues reported, cult members who previously had shown no interest in proselytizing now put their energies into gaining converts. They became even more committed to their cause after seeing what any reasonable person would conclude was shattering proof that they had been completely wrong.

Why should this be? The reason, Festinger tells us, is that it is psychologically painful to be confronted with information that contradicts what we believe. For Mrs. Keech's followers to concede error would have meant admitting they had been colossal fools. But convincing others of their beliefs would not only avoid any such embarrassment, it would provide some false comfort, as though more believers would constitute more proof.

The Keech cult is an extreme case, but the discomfort at being confronted with evidence of error is a universal human emotion. It's just no fun to admit we've been wrong. So we strive to avoid that unpleasant feeling of psychological conflict—what Festinger calls cognitive dissonance—that occurs when deeply held beliefs are challenged by conflicting evidence. Keech's followers could have reduced their dissonance by abandoning their religious beliefs, but instead some of them adopted an explanation of the new evidence that was compatible with what they already believed. Cognitive dissonance is a fancy term for something all of us feel from time to time. Decades of social science experiments have shown that, in a sense, there's a little UFO cultist in everybody.

The Moonbat Effect

A more recent example took place in 2006 when a website called truthout.org reported the political equivalent of a UFO landing that didn't happen. On Saturday, May 13, the truthout contributor Jason Leopold reported that President Bush's top political adviser, Karl Rove, had been indicted for perjury and lying to investigators in a CIA leak investigation, that Rove's lawyer had been served with the indictment papers during a fifteen-hour meeting at his law offices the previous day, and that the prosecutor would announce the charges publicly within a week. All this was reported as fact, without any "maybes" or qualifications.

The news was celebrated by followers of truthout, a liberal, anti-Bush site. One commenter on the website's "Town Meeting" message board even suggested a war crimes trial, saying "How about sending him and his bosses to The Hague?" Another gloated, "All that needs to be done now is to send him to the crossbar hotel, under the loving care of Bubba & No-Neck." The fact that no major news organization was reporting the Rove indictment was brushed off as evidence of the supposed pro-Bush, antiliberal bias of the "MSM" or mainstream media.

But the story quickly drew strong denials. Rove's lawyer said he, the lawyer, was out of his office that day taking his sick cat to the veterinarian and certainly hadn't been served with an indictment. Days passed with no indictment announced, and on Thursday truthout's executive director, Marc Ash, said that "additional sources have now come forward and offered corroboration to us." At the end of the week in which the indictment was supposed to be announced, Ash issued a "partial apology," but only about the timing: "We erred in getting too far out in front of the news-cycle." He kept the original story on the website. On May 25 Ash wrote, "We have now three independent sources confirming that attorneys for Karl Rove were handed an indictment." On June 3 he wrote, "We stand by the story." And still no indictment.

A number of readers expressed disappointment but others seemed to cling even more firmly to their now discredited editor and reporter's story. "Mr. Leopold's version may have been perfectly correct but changed by subsequent events he was not privy to," wrote one, posting a comment on truthout's "Town Meeting" message board. Another wrote, "No apology needed. I am glad you took the risk and you confirmed my faith in you." Still another wrote, "Persevere, keep the faith and above all keep up the good work. You can expect my contribution next week." Even when Rove's lawyer finally announced on June 13 that the special prosecutor had informed him that Rove wasn't going to be indicted, a diehard few continued to believe truthout. "I know that I trust their word over what the media says," one supporter wrote. Ash still kept the indictment story on the website and said of Rove's lawyer, "We question his motives."

However, by this time most of the comments on the "Town Meeting" board reflected a view of reporter Leopold and editor Ash as doggedly self-deceived, or worse. One wrote, "I've been on your side all along and am a great believer in TO [truthout], but this borders on lunacy." And another said, "There's probably a 12 step program out there for this affliction. You believe, with all your heart, soul, mind and body that a story is correct. You base your belief, not on evidence, logic or reason, but simply because you want to believe so badly, the thought of it being wrong invalidates your very existence and that makes your head hurt." That didn't please truthout's proprietors, who removed the comment. But it describes the effects of cognitive dissonance pretty well.

Extreme political partisans sometimes display such irrational thinking that they have come to be dismissed as "barking moonbats." A barking moonbat is "someone who sacrifices sanity for the sake of consistency," according to the London blogger Adriana Cronin-Lukas of Samizdata.net, who helped popularize the colorful phrase. It is most often applied derisively to extreme partisans on the left, but we use it as originally intended, to apply to all farout cases whose beliefs make them oblivious to facts, regardless of party or ideology.

The Psychology of Deception

In the past half century, the science of psychology has taught us a lot about how and why we get things wrong. As we'll see, our minds betray us not only when it comes to politics, but in all sorts of matters, from how we see a sporting event, or even a war, to the way we process a sales pitch. Humans are not by nature the fact-driven, rational beings we like to think we are. We get the facts wrong more often than we think we do. And we do so in predictable ways: we engage in wishful thinking. We embrace information that supports our beliefs and reject evidence that challenges them. Our minds tend to take shortcuts, which require some effort to avoid. Only a few of us go to moonbat extremes, but more often than most of us would imagine, the human mind operates in ways that defy logic.

Psychological experiments have shown, for one thing, that humans tend to seek out even weak evidence to support their existing beliefs, and to ignore evidence that undercuts those beliefs. In the process, we apply stringent tests to evidence we don't want to hear, while letting slide uncritically into our minds any information that suits our needs. Psychology also tells us that we rarely work through reasons and evidence in a systematic way, weighing information carefully and suspending the impulse to draw conclusions. Instead, much of the time we use mental shortcuts or rules of thumb that save us mental effort. These habits often work reasonably well, but they also can lead us to conclusions we might dismiss if we applied more thought.

Another common psychological trap is that we tend to overgeneralize from vivid, dramatic single examples. News of a terrible airline crash makes us think of commercial flying as dangerous; we forget that more than 10 million airline passenger flights land safely every year in the United States alone. Overhyped coverage of a few dramatic crimes on the local news makes us leap to the conclusion that crime is rampant, even when a look at some hard statistics would convince us that the violent crime rate in 2005 (despite a small increase that year) was actually 38 percent *lower* than its peak in 1991.

Psychologists have also found that when we feel most strongly that we are right, we may in fact be wrong. And they have found that people making an argument or a supposedly factual claim can manipulate us by the words they choose and the way they present their case. We can't avoid letting language do our thinking for us, but we can become more aware of how and when language is steering us toward a conclusion that, upon reflection, we might choose to reject. In this chapter we'll describe ways in which we get spun, and how to avoid the psychological pitfalls that lead us to ignore facts or believe bad information.

And this has nothing to do with intelligence. Presidents, poets, and even professors and journalists fall into these traps. You do it. We all do it. But we are less likely to do it if we learn to recognize how our minds can trick us, and learn to step around the mental snares nature has set for us. The late Amos Tversky, a psychologist who pioneered the study of decision errors in the 1970s, frequently said, "Whenever there is a simple error that most laymen fall for, there is always a slightly more sophisticated version of the same problem that experts fall for."*

Experts such as the doctors, lawyers, and college professors who made up a group convened in 1988 by Kathleen Jamieson to study the impact of political ads. They all thought other people were being fooled by advertising, but that they themselves were not. They were asked, "What effect, if any, do you think the presidential ads are having on voters in general and us in particular?" Every person in the group said that voters were being manipulated. But each one also insisted that he or she was invulnerable to persuasion by ads. Then the discussion moved on to the question "What ads have you seen in the past week?" One participant recounted that he had seen an ad on Democratic presidential candidate Michael Dukakis's "revolving-door prison policy." The group then spent time talking about Dukakis's policies on crime control, and in that discussion each adopted the language used in the Republican ad. The ad's language had begun to do their thinking about Dukakis for them. Without being aware of it, they had absorbed and embraced the metaphor that Dukakis had installed a "revolving door" on state prisons. The notion that others will be affected by exposure to messages while we are immune is called the third-person effect.

The other side of the third-person effect is wishful thinking. Why do most people think they are more likely than they actually are to live past eighty? Why do most believe that they are better than average drivers? At times we all seem to live in Garrison Keillor's fictional Lake Wobegon, where "all the children are above average." To put it differently: in some matters we are unrealistic about how unrealistic we actually are.

---

* Famous people often are misquoted (see "False Quotes" box on page 147), but this quote is genuine. Tversky's collaborator, Nobel Prize–winning Princeton professor Daniel Kahneman, told us that both he and Tversky often repeated the remark in conversation and that Tversky probably came up with it first.

The "Pictures in Our Heads" Trap

Misinformation is easy to accept if it reinforces what we already be-lieve. The journalist Walter Lippman observed in 1922 that we are all captives of the "pictures in our heads," which don't always con-form to the real world. "The way in which the world is imagined de-termines at any particular moment what men will do," Lippman wrote in his book *Public Opinion*. Deceivers are aware of the human tendency to think in terms of stereotypes, and they exploit it.

A good example of this is the way the Bush campaign in 2004 got away with falsely accusing John Kerry of repeatedly trying to raise gasoline taxes and of favoring a 50-cent increase at a time when fuel prices were soaring. A typical ad said, "He supported higher gasoline taxes eleven times." In fact, Kerry had voted for a single 4.3-cent increase, in 1993. The following year, he flirted briefly in a newspaper interview with the idea of a 50-cent-a-gallon gasoline tax, but quickly dropped the notion and never mentioned it again. Nevertheless, most voters swallowed the Republican false-hood without a hiccup.

Democrats exploit this psychological trap, too. In the previous chapter we noted how Kerry had falsely accused Bush of favor-ing big "cuts" in Social Security benefits. That was also widely be-lieved. In the National Annenberg Election Survey, nearly half of respondents—49 percent—tended to believe a statement that Bush's plan would "cut Social Security benefits 30 to 45 percent." Only 37 percent found the statement untruthful. And we want to stress an important point here: the public wasn't thinking of a "cut" as a slowdown in the growth of benefits for those retiring decades in the future; they were thinking of a real cut. The Annenberg survey found that 50 percent rated as truthful a statement that "Bush's plan to cut Social Security would cut benefits for those cur-rently receiving them," and only 43 percent found the statement untruthful.

Bush, of course, had stated repeatedly during his 2000 campaign and throughout his first term that he would not cut current benefits by a penny. So why would a plurality of the public believe the opposite? The reason, we believe, is that Social Security is thought of as a Democratic program and Republicans are thought of as opposing it (somewhat unfairly: large majorities of Republican House and Senate members voted for it when it was passed in 1935). Because of the stereotyped view that Republicans don't favor Social Security, too few took the trouble to question the idea that Bush would cut current benefits.

It is difficult for candidates to overcome these stereotypes. In 1990, voters in Pennsylvania were disposed to believe that the Republican nominee, Barbara Hafer, opposed abortion rights and that the incumbent Democratic governor, Robert Casey, favored a legal right to abortion; the reverse was true. In general, Democrats are more likely to be "pro-choice" and Republicans "pro-life," but not in this case. A good rule is that "in general" doesn't necessarily apply to "this specific."

Sometimes we have to avoid mental shortcuts and take the long way around if we want to avoid being manipulated or making these mistakes on our own. Ask yourself: "Is the picture in my head a good likeness of reality? Does this Democrat in fact favor this tax increase? Does this Republican in fact want to cut Social Security benefits? Where's the evidence?"

The "Root for My Side" Trap

Related to the "pictures in our heads" trap is the "root for my side" trap. There's evidence that our commitment to a cause not only colors our thinking but also affects what we see—and don't see as we observe the world around us.

Psychologists have known about this phenomenon for a long time. In 1954, Albert Hastorf and Hadley Cantril published a classic study of how Princeton and Dartmouth football fans saw a penalty-ridden game in which the Princeton quarterback was taken

off the field with a broken nose and a mild concussion and a Dartmouth player later suffered a broken leg. They found that 86 percent of the Princeton students said that Dartmouth started the
rough play, but only 36 percent of the Dartmouth students saw it
that way. The researchers asked, "Do you believe the game was
clean and fairly played or that it was unnecessarily rough and dirty?"
The results: 93 percent of Princeton fans said "rough and dirty," compared with only 42 percent of Dartmouth fans. When shown films
of the game and asked to count actual infractions by Dartmouth
players, Princeton students spotted an average of 9.8, twice as many
as the 4.3 infractions noted by Dartmouth students.

Were the Dartmouth and Princeton fans deliberately distorting
what they saw? Probably not. Hastorf and Cantril went so far as to
say that people don't just have different attitudes about things, they
actually see different things: "For the 'thing' simply is *not* the same
for different people whether the 'thing' is a football game, a presidential candidate, Communism or spinach."

We don't know about spinach, but when it comes to presidential candidates a recent study using brain-scanning technology
supports the notion that people really do see things differently, de-
pending on whom they back. The scans also suggest that emotion
takes over and logic doesn't come into play. (See "This is your brain
on politics" box.)

A closely related effect is what researchers call the hostile
media phenomenon. Three Stanford University researchers
demonstrated this in 1985 by showing pro-Arab and pro-Israeli audiences identical news accounts of the massacre of several hundred persons in the Sabra and Shatila refugee camps near Beirut,
Lebanon, in 1982. Each side detected more negative than positive
references to their side, and each side thought the coverage was
likely to sway neutral observers in a direction hostile to them. Why?
Probably because content that agrees with our own views simply
seems true and thus not very noteworthy, while material that counters our biases stands out in our minds and makes us look for a

This Is Your Brain on Politics

During the 2004 presidential campaign, the Emory University psychologist Drew Westen and his colleagues conducted brain scans of fifteen Bush supporters and fifteen Kerry supporters, who were asked to evaluate statements attributed to each candidate. The researchers told the subjects that Kerry had reversed his position on overhauling Social Security, and they said Bush flip-flopped on his support for the former chief executive of Enron, Ken Lay.

Not surprisingly, each group judged the other's candidate harshly but let its own candidate off fairly easy—clear evidence of bias. More interesting was what the brain scans showed. "We did not see any increased activation of the parts of the brain normally engaged during reasoning," Westen said in announcing his results. "What we saw instead was a network of emotion circuits lighting up."

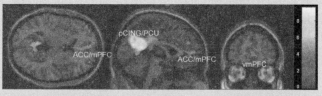

Fig. 1: Emotional centers active when processing information unfavorable to the partisan's preferred candidate

Furthermore, after the partisans had come to conclusions favorable to their candidates, their brain scans showed activity in circuits associated with reward, rather as the brains of addicts do when they get a fix. "Essentially, it appears as if partisans twirl the cognitive kaleidoscope until they get the conclusions they want, and then they get massively reinforced for it," Westen said.

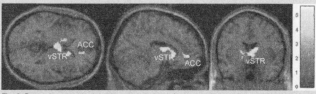

Fig. 2. Reward centers active when processing information that gets the partisan's preferred candidate off the hook

Westen's experiment supplies physical evidence that emotionally biased thinking may be hard-wired into our brains.

reason to reject it. So, to a conservative, news with a conservative slant is fair; to a liberal, news with a liberal slant is fair; and to both, there is something unfair somewhere in any news program that tries to balance alternative points of view.

Psychologists call this phenomenon confirmation bias, and it not only colors how we see things, but how we reason as well. David Perkins, a professor of education at Harvard, has aptly called it "myside bias." In studies of how people reason when asked to think about a controversial issue, Perkins observed a strong tendency for people to come up with reasons favoring their own side, and not even to think about reasons favoring the other. His test subjects offered three times more considerations on their own side of an issue as they did against their position, and that count included arguments they brought up just for the sake of shooting them down.

The University of Pennsylvania psychologist Jonathan Baron found a classic example of myside bias in a *Daily Pennsylvanian* student article in favor of abortion rights, which said: "If government rules against abortion, it will be acting contrary to one of the basic rights of Americans, . . . the right to make decisions for oneself." The author of that sentence was oblivious to the thought that the other side sees abortion as equivalent to murder, and that laws against homicide also interfere with "the right to make decisions for oneself" when the decision is to commit murder.

When Baron asked fifty-four University of Pennsylvania students to prepare for a discussion of the morality of abortion, he found, as expected, that they tended to list arguments on only one side of the question. What was even more revealing, the students who made one-sided arguments also rated the arguments of others as being of better quality when those other arguments were all on one side, too, even arguments on the opposing side. He concluded: "People consider one-sided thinking to be better than two-sided thinking, even for forming one's own opinion on an issue."

General Norman Schwarzkopf fell into the confirmation bias

trap after leading U.S. forces to one of the most lopsided military victories in history during the Gulf War in 1991. As Colin Powell tells it in his autobiography, *My American Journey,* Schwarzkopf appeared at a news conference with video that he said showed a U.S. smart bomb hitting Iraqi Scud missile launchers. When Powell informed him that an analyst had identified the targets as fuel trucks, not missile launchers, Schwarzkopf exploded. "By God, those certainly were Scuds. That analyst doesn't know what he's talking about. He's just not as good as the others." Powell says later examination showed that the analyst was right. Schwarzkopf just couldn't see it. Believing that his forces were really hitting Scud launchers, he was open only to evidence that confirmed his belief.

Even scholars are affected by this powerful bias. In the 1980s, the National Institute of Education (NIE) asked six scholars to conduct an analysis of existing research into the effects of desegregated schools. Two of the scholars were thought to favor school integration, two to oppose it, and two to be neither opponents nor proponents. Sure enough, the differences in their findings were consistent with their ideological predispositions. The differences were slight, which is a testament to the power of the scientific method to rein in bias. But the bias was there nonetheless.

Once you know about confirmation bias, it is easy to detect in others. Confirmation bias was at work when CIA analysts rejected evidence that Iraq had really destroyed its chemical and biological weapons and gave weight only to signs that Saddam Hussein retained hidden stockpiles. Confirmation bias explains why so many people believe in psychics and astrologers: they register only the apparently accurate predictions and ignore those that miss. Confirmation bias explains why, once someone has made a bad first impression on a date or during a job interview, that impression is so hard to live down. And it is because of confirmation bias that good scientists try actively to *disprove* their own theories: otherwise, it would be just too easy to see only the supporting evidence.

To avoid this psychological trap, apply a bit of the scientific method to political claims and marketing messages. When they sound good, ask yourself what fact could prove them untrue and what evidence you may be failing to consider. You may find that a partisan or dogmatic streak is keeping you from seeing facts clearly.

The "I Know I'm Right" Trap

There's evidence that the more misinformed we are, the more strongly we insist that we're correct. In a fascinating piece of research published in 2000, the political psychologist James H. Kuklinski and his colleagues reported findings from a random telephone survey of 1,160 Illinois residents. They found few who were very well informed about the facts of the welfare system: only 3 percent got more than half the questions right. That wasn't very surprising, but what should be a warning to us all is this: those holding the least accurate beliefs were the ones expressing the highest confidence in those beliefs.

Of those who said correctly that only 7 percent of American families were getting welfare, just under half said they were very confident or fairly highly confident of their answer. But 74 percent of those who grossly overestimated the percentage of those on welfare said they were very confident or fairly highly confident, even though the figure they gave (25 percent) was more than three times too high. This "I know I'm right" syndrome means that those who most need to revise the pictures in their heads are the very ones least likely to change their thinking. Of such people, it is sometimes said that they are "often in error but never in doubt."

The "Close Call" Trap

Psychological research shows that when we are confronted with tough decisions and close calls, we tend to exaggerate the differences. The psychologist Jack Brehm demonstrated this in a famous experiment published in 1956. He had women rate eight different products such as toasters and coffeemakers, then let them keep one—but allowed them to choose between only two of the products. He set up some of the decisions as "close calls," between two products the women had rated alike; others were easy calls, with wide differences in ratings. After the women had made their choices, Brehm asked them to rate the products again. This time, women who had been forced to make a tough choice tended to be more positive about the product they had picked and less positive about the one they had rejected. This change was less evident among women who had made the easy call.

Psychologists call this the "spreading of alternatives" effect, a natural human tendency to make ourselves feel better about the choices we have made, even at the expense of accuracy or consistency. We crave certainty, and don't want to agonize endlessly about whether we made the right call. This mental habit helps us avoid becoming frozen by indecision, but it also can make changing our minds harder than need be when the facts change, or when we have misread the evidence in the first place. Once in a while we need to ask, "Would I feel this way if I were buying this product (or hearing this argument) for the first time? Have new facts emerged since I made my initial decision?"

It's easy to fall into traps like the ones we've described here, because people manage most of the time on automatic pilot, using mental shortcuts without really having to think everything through constantly. Consider a famous experiment published by the Harvard psychologist Ellen Langer in 1978. She and her colleagues repeatedly attempted to cut in front of persons about to use a university copying machine. To some they said, "Excuse me. May I use the Xerox machine, because I'm in a rush?" They were allowed to cut in 94 percent of the time. To others, the cheeky researchers said only, "Excuse me. May I use the Xerox machine?," without giving any reason. These succeeded only 60 percent of the time. So far, that's what you would probably expect: we're likelier to accommodate someone who has a good reason for a request than someone who just wants to push ahead for their own personal convenience. But here's the illuminating point: Langer showed that giving an obviously bogus reason worked just as well as giving a good one. When Langer's cohorts said, "Excuse me, may I use the Xerox machine, because I have to make some copies?" they were allowed to cut in 93 percent of the time.

"Because I have to make some copies" is really no reason at all, of course. Langer's conclusion is that her unwitting test subjects reacted to the word "because" without really listening to or thinking about the reason being offered; they were in a state she called "mindlessness."

Others have demonstrated the same zombielike tendency, even among university students who supposedly are smarter than average. Robert Levine, a psychology professor at California State University, Fresno, tried different pitches during a campus bake sale. Asking "Would you like to buy a cookie?" resulted in purchases by only two out of thirty passersby. But his researchers sold six times more cookies when they asked "Would you like to buy a cookie? It's for a good cause." Of the thirty passersby who were asked that question, twelve bought cookies. And none even bothered to ask what the "good cause" was.

Marketers use the insights from such studies against us. An Internet-based salesman named Alexi Neocleous tells potential clients that Langer's study shows "because" is "a magic word [that] literally forces people to buckle at the knees and succumb to your offer." He adds, "The lesson for you is, give your prospects the reason why, no matter how stupid it may seem to YOU!"

The lesson we should draw as consumers and citizens is just the opposite: watch out for irrelevant or nonexistent reasons, and make important decisions attentively. "Mindlessness" and reliance on mental shortcuts are often fine; we probably won't go far wrong buying the most popular brand of soap or toothpaste even if "bestselling" doesn't really mean "best." Often the most popular brand is as good a choice as any other. But when we're deciding on big-ticket items, it pays to switch on our brains and think a bit harder.

How can we break the spell? Research shows that when people are forced to "counterargue"—to express the other side's point of view as well as their own—they are more likely to accept new evidence rather than reject it. Try what Jonathan Baron, of the University of Pennsylvania, calls active open-mindedness. Baron recommends putting initial impressions to the test by seeking evidence against them as well as evidence in their favor. "When we find alternatives or counterevidence we must weigh it fairly," he says in his book *Judgment Misguided*. "Of course, there may sometimes be no 'other side,' or it may be so evil or foolish that we can dismiss it quickly. But if we are not open to it, we will never know."

That makes sense to us. We need to ask ourselves, "Are there facts I don't know about because I haven't looked for them? What am I missing here?" Otherwise, we're liable to end up like Mrs. Keech's UFO cultists, preaching with utter conviction that Guardians from the Planet Clarion really do exist, or like the blustering General Schwarzkopf angrily denying the truth about those burned-out tanker trucks. It's better to be aware of our own psychology, to know that our brains tend to "light up" to reinforce our existing beliefs when we hear our favorite candidates or positions challenged. To avoid being deceived (or deceiving ourselves) we have to make sure the pictures in our heads come as close to reflecting the world outside as they reasonably can.

THE JUST WAR THEORY

Chapter 5

Facts Can
Save Your Life

GETTING THE FACTS RIGHT IS IMPORTANT. IT CAN SAVE YOUR money, your health, even your freedom.

We're not exaggerating one bit. Consider the story of Daniel Bullock, a California physician who got spun by a sleazy tax-shelter promoter and then received some unwelcome visitors carrying badges and guns. "My seventeen-year-old daughter answered the door to some armed federal agents from the [IRS] criminal investigation division," he recalled. "That was a bad day." And worse followed: Bullock lost his medical license and served eight months in a federal prison camp, all because he had failed to check the facts when a smooth-talking promoter sold him what turned out to be a criminal tax-evasion scam.

Bullock was a churchgoing orthopedic surgeon from Mount Shasta, California, who did volunteer work in Central America. But like a lot of people, he hated paying his taxes, and resented the stories he had heard about how others avoided taxes entirely. "When I encountered someone with 'inside information' on how the very wealthy avoid taxes I was all ears," Bullock told a Senate subcommittee in 2002, after he had started serving his sentence. "He had a good story, a well used and 'successful' strategy, hundreds of clients and legal opinions in support of his program." Bullock fell into the "I don't want to hear it" trap. He was so convinced that his benefactor had discovered a legal way to avoid paying taxes that he failed to look for evidence to the contrary.

Bullock bought into a preposterous scheme that sent his earnings on a round trip to the Caribbean through a series of offshore banks and "nonprofit" trusts. These entities returned the money to him by paying his mortgage and other personal living expenses. That made Bullock's money hard for the IRS to trace but did nothing to erase his legal obligation to pay taxes on it. It was just a scam, as was clear to Bullock's bookkeeper, who eventually turned him in to the IRS. The judge who sentenced Bullock thought it should have been apparent to anybody. "Any ten-year-old would know this was obviously illegal," he said.

Bullock might have avoided prison by practicing a little "active open-mindedness" and asking himself how likely it was that the IRS would actually allow this kind of dodge. He might also have called someone who didn't stand to make money on the scheme, unlike the promoter who collected thousands of dollars in fees for his "services." Bullock's own lawyer or accountant might have quickly set him straight about what a dim view the IRS takes of sham transactions and international money-laundering. Bullock might also have conducted a quick Internet search on the name of the promoter who sold him the scheme, which might have turned up the fact that the man had already been convicted on seven counts of aiding and assisting the filing of false tax returns. Today, a simple search for the term "tax schemes" brings up page after page of official warnings about similar scams and the prosecutions that often result. Try it yourself.

Bullock's story shows that letting bad information go unchallenged can have grave consequences. He is not alone. Thousands of people have used tax-evasion schemes like the one he fell for, and while most don't go to prison they all risk being forced to pay fines, big penalties, and interest on top of the back taxes when they are caught. Some may know they are engaging in criminal activity, but we suspect the majority are like Bullock, actively obtuse when it comes to matters that improve their tax returns. And it hardly matters whether we have been deceived by somebody else or have failed to check out our own dubious assumptions. The price for getting the facts wrong is the same whether we are deceived or self-deceived, misinformed or disinformed, spun by others or spun by the pictures in our head. The message here is simple: facts matter.

The "Grey Goose Effect"

Most bad information won't land you in jail or ruin your career, but much of it will cost you money. For proof of that, look no further than the snake-oil hustles we mentioned in Chapter 1. We can be manipulated into spending too much money in more subtle ways, too. For example, we tend to think of higher-priced goods as being of better quality than lower-priced goods; but while "You get what you pay for" may be common folk wisdom, it isn't always true. In the 1950s, Pepsi competed with Coca-Cola by selling its soda at half the price of Coke and advertising "twice as much for a nickel." But more people bought Pepsi after it *raised* its price, a lesson not lost on other marketers. A formerly obscure brand of Scotch whiskey also increased its sales by raising its price, giving its name to what is now known as the Chivas Regal effect.

Today it might better be called the Grey Goose effect, after the hot-selling French vodka that came on the U.S. market in 1997 selling for $27 a bottle, nearly triple the price of the top-of-the-market Smirnoff brand. Grey Goose sales exploded. Vodka is officially defined by U.S. government regulations as "neutral spirits . . . without distinctive character, aroma, or taste," so it is hard to see how one vodka can be three times better than another on any objective basis. The drink is basically distilled alcohol cut with water.

Now, when our sharp-eyed Random House editor, Tim Bartlett, first saw this he objected: "Expensive vodkas on average are significantly smoother than cheap ones, which taste like rubbing alcohol." We're quite sure that's how it seems to Tim and many others, but they're not judging only on the basis of what their taste buds tell them. They are also taking into account, perhaps unconsciously, the price they have paid for the vodka, the amount of advertising they have seen telling them that the expensive vodka is superior and is drunk by sophisticated, in-the-know people, and even the fancy design of the bottle. We might agree that the Grey Goose bottle is prettier than the Smirnoff bottle, but that has nothing to do with what the bottles contain. Try comparing brands without any predisposition to think one is better than the other, and see what happens. The New York City artist (and blogger) Andrea Harner did just that. She and her husband, Jonah Peretti, invited over some friends in March 2006 for a blindfold test comparing Smirnoff to Grey Goose. Result: eight of sixteen correctly picked which was which. That's exactly 50 percent, the same result you would expect from tossing a coin. Harner's testers did much better telling regular Coke from regular Pepsi: 70 percent got the cola right.

Taste is subjective, and you might well conclude that the illusion of better taste is worth paying for. Or perhaps your palate is more sensitive than the palates of Ms. Harner and her friends. Our point is, simply, that higher price predisposes us to think that a product is better, even when it's not. With respect to vodka, soda, or any other beverage, you can't know for sure what really tastes better unless you do a blindfold test yourself. As Ms. Harner wrote: "The point is that this challenge was A LOT harder than people expected. A LOT. I dare you to give it a try." At the very least, her test results suggest you could pour Smirnoff into a Grey Goose bottle and your friends would never know the difference.

The price-equals-quality fallacy is exploited by others besides the booze industry. Many second-tier private colleges and universities make sure the "sticker price" of their tuition is close to (or even higher than) Harvard's, Princeton's, and Yale's, in the hope that parents and students will take the mental shortcut of equating price with quality. *Consumer Reports* magazine, which conducts carefully designed tests on all sorts of products from automobiles to toasters to TV sets, often finds lower-priced goods to be of higher quality than those costing much more. For example, in a comparison of upright vacuum cleaners on the magazine's website in 2006, the $140 Eureka Boss Smart Vac Ultra 4870 was rated better overall than the $1,330 Kirby Ultimate G Diamond Edition or the $700 Oreck XL21-700. The Eureka was better than the highly advertised $500 Dyson DC15. Dyson claims that its vacuum "never lose[s] suction," and maybe that's true. But the independent testers at *Consumer Reports* found that the Eureka did a better job of cleaning carpets, at less than a third the price.

The mismatch between price and quality has been apparent for a long time. Back in 1979, the University of Iowa business professor Peter C. Riesz checked the *Consumer Reports* ratings of 679 different packaged foods over fifteen years. He found that the correlation between quality and price "is near zero." In other words, price had very little if anything to do with quality; the cheaper product was the better one about half the time.

So don't get spun by price tags. Shop around, and keep in mind that sometimes less expensive options are good enough, and in some cases just as good as the pricier alternative. It pays to check the facts.

Selling False Hope

Getting facts wrong not only can cost you money or get you in trouble with the law: it can put you in the hospital, or worse. Consider the harrowing story of a cancer patient named Chuck Hysong, of

Hendersonville, North Carolina. According to his wife, Pamela, he'd been improving while taking a new medication prescribed by his oncologist. But at nine P.M. on April 12, 2002, he took a preparation called Optimizer ENG-C, sold to him by a man recommended by a relative who was skeptical of doctors and a believer in "alternative" medicine.

Mrs. Hysong says she had begged her husband not to take the "optimizer" preparation. For one thing, the man who sold it "told my husband that he has a 100 percent cure rate for bone cancer," Mrs. Hysong recalls. That was obviously too good to be true, and there were other clear warning signs. The seller refused to list the ingredients of his "supplements," Mrs. Hysong says, adding that he also demanded $5,000 payment, in advance, not covered by any medical insurance. She refused to pay, but the relative put up the first $2,000. "Chuck was desperate," Mrs. Hysong recalls. "He was still a relatively young man, and he wasn't ready to go, and he was ready to try anything within what he considered reason." That's typical of many seriously ill people for whom science offers little hope; they fall prey to quackery and medical fraud, losing money and sometimes suffering further damage to their health.

Mrs. Hysong describes what happened when her husband took the $2,000 Optimizer preparation:

"By nine-thirty, he had uncontrollable diarrhea; almost constant discharge from his nose; he was hallucinating that he had smoke coming off his body; he was burning hot; he made uncontrollable noises; he was nauseated; he was scared; and he was angry. After about an hour of diarrhea, when he tried to stand, he could not do so without bracing himself. He could not walk back to bed."

Mr. Hysong was rushed to the hospital, where he spent the night. He was left "dehydrated, weak, and ashamed that he had been sucked into this," according to his wife. His earlier improvement ceased. "About a week later he started going south again," Mrs. Hysong said. "I don't know if it was coincidence, or the stress to his body." Chuck Hysong died three months later. Cancer killed him, but as Mrs. Hysong describes it, the pills added to his suffering and weakened him in his final days.

The red flags still fly. Robert Dowling, the man Mrs. Hysong says sold the pills to her husband, runs something he calls the North Carolina Institute of Technology. Though he claims no formal medical training, in 2006 his website—www.cancercured.org— claimed to have a method of finding and curing breast cancer before it develops. Dowling had done business in South Carolina before coming north, but South Carolina authorities shut down his operation in September 2001 after the death of a client, a seventy-one-year-old woman suffering from stomach cancer. A few months earlier, the U.S. Food and Drug Administration had warned Dowling that he was illegally selling an unapproved medical device by marketing "Bioscan 2010" home kits, which could supposedly predict disease. Dowling moved on to an even smaller town, giving his address as Hot Springs, North Carolina.

What Really Kills Women?

Far more lethal than any quack healer, however, is the misinformation about our bodies and our health that millions of us carry around unquestioned. As recently as 1997, for example, adult women and men were most likely to name breast cancer as the leading killer of women, which isn't close to being true and never has been. The plain fact is women are *nine times* more likely to die of heart disease, and more than twice as likely to die from stroke. Lung cancer kills far more women than breast cancer, and so do other chronic lung diseases, such as emphysema. Furthermore, many of these deaths could be avoided if women had a more accurate mental picture of their true health risks and acted accordingly.

To be sure, the attention to breast cancer has done a great deal of good, making women more likely to detect cancers at a curable stage through regular mammograms and self-examinations. That's one reason breast cancer deaths have been declining. But the hard facts imply that women should be many times more concerned about heart attacks, stroke, and lung disease than about breast cancer. They should educate themselves about the warning signs of heart attack (these signs are somewhat different in women than in men, by the way), and consider preventive diet and exercise habits. For the millions of women who smoke, the facts might convince them to try quitting. Everybody knows smoking increases the risk of lung disease and heart attack, but a more accurate picture of how *many* women die from these could provide smokers with added motivation to drop the habit. In short, facts can save lives.

It's easy to see why so many had the wrong idea, not because of any intentional deception but because breast cancer gets enormous attention in the news media and that's where most people get their information. When a CBS/*New York Times* poll asked people where they learned most about health-related issues, only one in ten said from a doctor; six in ten said they learned most from television, newspapers, or magazines. However, what reporters and editors

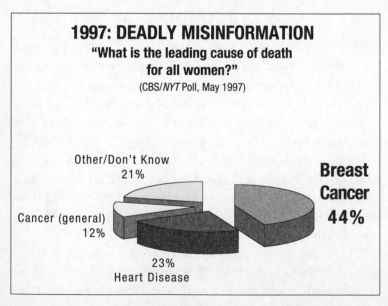

1997: DEADLY MISINFORMATION
"What is the leading cause of death
for all women?"
(CBS/*NYT* Poll, May 1997)

Other/Don't Know
21%

Breast
Cancer
44%

Cancer (general)
12%

23%
Heart Disease

find newsworthy often is a poor measure of what people really need to know. We get spun by mistaking how often we hear about something for how often it really occurs. For example, as we've already mentioned, the more crime stories people see on TV, the more crime-ridden they believe their communities to be, even when crime is declining. Psychologists call this effect the availability heuristic, a mental bias that gives more weight to vividness and emotional impact than to actual probability.

Ironically, breast cancer gets so much attention partly because so many women *survive* it and become advocates, producing and participating in publicity-grabbing events such as the annual Race for the Cure. That's not a bad thing, as we've noted. But the deadlier risks deserve even more publicity and attention.

A poll taken in March 2005 showed 55 percent of women correctly identified heart disease as their leading killer. The percentage of respondents who get this question right had doubled since 1997. But that change required a massive campaign by the federal government as well as the American Heart Association and other groups. First Lady Laura Bush made women's heart disease a

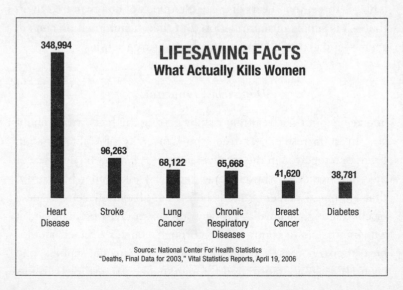

LIFESAVING FACTS
What Actually Kills Women

Heart Disease	Stroke	Lung Cancer	Chronic Respiratory Diseases	Breast Cancer	Diabetes
348,994	96,263	68,122	65,668	41,620	38,781

Source: National Center For Health Statistics
"Deaths, Final Data for 2003," Vital Statistics Reports, April 19, 2006

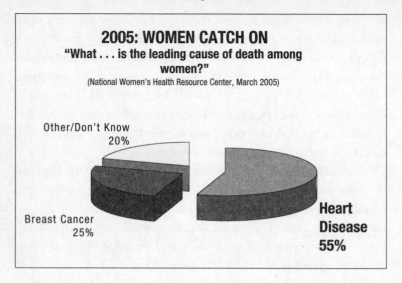

2005: WOMEN CATCH ON
"What . . . is the leading cause of death among women?"
(National Women's Health Resource Center, March 2005)

Other/Don't Know 20%

Breast Cancer 25%

Heart Disease 55%

personal project, and the government's National Heart, Lung, and Blood Institute scored big in 2003 with its "Red Dress Project," hooking up with the glitzy Mercedes Benz Fashion Week and nineteen designers. Yet 25 percent of women still think breast cancer is a bigger threat than heart disease. No quack or con man told them that—it is simple misinformation. But that misinformation can kill them—and getting the facts straight can save their lives.

Dangerous Ignorance

Teenagers put their health at risk by getting the facts wrong about sex. In 2005 researchers from the University of California–San Francisco reported in the medical journal *Pediatrics* on a survey of 580 ninth-graders, whose average age was just under fifteen. Of that group, 14 percent stated there was "absolutely zero chance" of contracting chlamydia through oral sex, and 13 percent said it was impossible to contract HIV through oral sex. In fact, studies have shown herpes, hepatitis, gonorrhea, chlamydia, syphilis, and even HIV can be transmitted through oral sex, the study's authors said. Here, ignorance can lead to a nasty infection or even a life-threatening disease.

Figures from the same study illustrate another type of dangerous sexual ignorance: teens thought others were having sex far more than was actually the case. Only 13.5 percent of the ninth-graders said they had experienced vaginal sex, for example, but the group estimated that 41 percent of others their age had done so—three times the actual number. So it's probably no coincidence that 26 percent said they intended to have vaginal sex soon, within the next six months—double the percentage that had already experienced it. Peer pressure and peer acceptance are important to adolescents, so thinking that three times as many of their peers are having sex as is really the case probably leads some to try it who might not if they knew the truth.

A similar ignorance prevails among college students. A 2003 study at Virginia's James Madison University surveyed attitudes about casual sexual behavior while "hooking up"—on a first date with no future commitment. Students were asked how comfortable they felt about engaging in a variety of acts during a hookup, from petting above the waist to sexual intercourse. "Our study suggests that men believe women are more comfortable engaging in these behaviors than in fact they are, and also that women believe other women are more comfortable engaging in these behaviors than they are themselves," the authors said. "As a consequence, some men may pressure women to engage in intimate sexual behaviors, and some women may engage in these behaviors or resist only weakly because they believe they are unique in feeling discomfort about engaging in them."

In other words, if teens and college students got their facts straight about what others were really doing and how those others really felt, fewer might feel pressured to have sex. Unwanted pregnancies, sexually transmitted diseases, and even sexual assaults could well decline.

Psychologists call this gap between perception and facts pluralistic ignorance, and it doesn't apply only to sex. Consider heavy drinking, for example: college students tend to think others are more comfortable with it than is actually the case. Studies suggest that male students, especially, may become heavy drinkers because they think—wrongly—that it's expected. Some college campuses are trying a campaign called Most of Us to provide students with statistical evidence about the true attitudes of their peers regarding booze, in the hope that abuse of alcohol will decline when those with more cautious attitudes realize they are in the majority.

Killer Facts

What you don't know can kill you. But some life-saving information is on the way.

Federal health researchers estimate that 125 to 150 persons die each year because of anaphylaxis caused by food allergies. They also estimate that 1 out of every 50 adults and 1 out of every 20 infants suffer to some degree from food allergies, which send an estimated 30,000 persons each year to hospital emergency rooms.

People don't always know what they're eating. An FDA survey in 1999 and 2000 found that 25 percent of sampled baked goods, ice cream, and candy contained peanuts or eggs although these were not included on the ingredients list. However, in January 2006 a new federal law took effect, the Food Allergen Labeling and Consumer Protection Act, which requires that manufacturers label for eight types of allergens that together account for 90 percent of allergic reactions: soybeans, eggs, milk, fish, wheat, peanuts, tree nuts (such as almonds and walnuts), and crustacean shellfish (such as shrimp and crab).

But be careful: the new law only applies to packaged foods, not to food sold by restaurants, neighborhood bakeries, kiosks, carry-out establishments, or street vendors.

Facts Change History

Misperceptions of the truth about majority opinion may even have held back the civil rights movement. In the 1960s, surveys showed Americans grossly underestimated the strength of public support for desegregation, even in the Deep South. One famous study, by the sociologist Hubert J. O'Gorman, showed that in 1968, for example, only one in three white Southerners said he or she actually favored segregation, but nearly two in three said they believed a majority of whites were segregationists. To put it another way, desegregationist whites were a big majority in the South but thought they were a minority. Would they have spoken up sooner and pushed their political leaders harder for more liberal civil rights and voting laws if they had known their own political strength? Would Alabama's George C. Wallace have carried five southern states in his 1968 presidential campaign had all whites known how others felt about segregation? We can never know for sure, but O'Gorman's study suggests that history might have been different if people hadn't been mistaken about how the majority felt.

We also have reason to speculate that mistaking the true attitudes of others might have contributed to the rash of business scandals and corporate crime that started coming to light in 2001. After the Enron scandal, a study conducted at the University of Oklahoma showed that lawyers think other lawyers are more likely to be unethical than they themselves are. Likewise, business students believed that businesspeople have less stringent ethical standards than their own. One implication, said the authors, is that "if they were to observe an ethical infraction, they might be less likely to speak up." Or, to turn that around, there might be more whistle-blowers and less corruption if more business executives and lawyers realized that the ethical standards of others aren't as lax as they suppose.

Fighting Words

Getting the facts wrong can—in fact, often does—lead to the worst of human calamities, war. The U.S.-led invasion of Iraq in 2003 is only the most recent example. Six weeks before it began, 76 percent of Americans in a *Time*/CNN/Harris Interactive poll answered "yes" when asked, "Do you think Saddam Hussein currently provides assistance to Osama bin Laden's Al-Qaeda terrorist network, or don't you think so?" Only 15 percent said "no." The widespread belief that Saddam was aiding Al-Qaeda was later declared un-founded by the bipartisan 9/11 Commission. Nothing that can fairly be called evidence has ever surfaced to support the notion. And of course, now we know that Saddam Hussein had dismantled his nu-clear weapons program and gotten rid of stockpiles of chemical and germ weapons, contrary to what the public was told by the presi-dent and the CIA before the war.

But the Iraq War isn't the first one Americans have fought on the basis of false beliefs. We've been making that mistake for more than a century.

On February 15, 1898, an explosion ripped through the hull of the American battleship U.S.S. *Maine* and sank her in Havana har-bor with the loss of 266 lives. Soon the cry "Remember the *Maine*, to Hell with Spain" was on the lips of war hawks; the incident led to the Spanish-American War and the loss of another 3,000 Ameri-can lives. But did the Spanish sink the *Maine*? Probably not.

Spain always denied any responsibility, and indeed had no sane reason to provoke the militarily superior Americans into a war that eventually cost it Cuba, the Philippines, Puerto Rico, and Guam. A century of historical inquiry has produced no documentary evi-dence of a Spanish plot. A mine might have been set by somebody else, perhaps a Cuban trying to provoke the United States into at-tacking Spain. But even that is now considered unlikely.

To be sure, two official naval inquiries, in 1898 and 1911, did conclude that the *Maine* was sunk by a mine. But in 1976, Admiral Hyman Rickover (the legendary officer who pushed through the development of the nuclear-powered submarine) conducted a pri-vate inquiry that concluded that the sinking was an accident. "We found no technical evidence . . . that an external explosion initiated the destruction of the *Maine*," Rickover wrote, adding, "The avail-able evidence is consistent with an internal explosion alone," prob-ably a coal fire that touched off a powder magazine. Coal fires, smoldering undetected, were a common hazard in the navies of that time.

Rickover's conclusion was questioned by a 1998 study commissioned by *National Geographic* magazine, using advanced computer modeling. But the study was inconclusive: "The sum of these findings is not definitive in proving that a mine was the cause of the sinking of the *Maine,* but it does strengthen the case in favor of a mine as the cause," the magazine said. Even that tentative statement was quickly contradicted by Otto P. Jons, executive vice president of Advanced Marine Enterprises, the very engineering company that conducted the *Geographic* study. Jons emphatically disagreed with his subordinates. "I am convinced it was not a mine," he said at a panel convened by the U.S. Naval Institute on April 22, 1998.

The United States has gone to war on the basis of false factual claims more than once since then. In August 1964, when President Lyndon Johnson asked Congress to give him practically unlimited authority to attack North Vietnam, he believed the enemy had attacked two American destroyers, the U.S.S. *Maddox* and the U.S.S. *Turner Joy,* on the night of August 4, 1964. We now know they hadn't. The *Maddox* had indeed been attacked the previous day, and there were bullet holes and photographs to prove it. But the second "attack" on the two ships was the result of jittery nerves and spurious readings of radar and sonar signals by U.S. sailors. Though the Navy claimed to have sunk two enemy PT boats during the second engagement, it never produced photographs, bodies, or wreckage to support that claim.

Later, a Navy pilot, James B. Stockdale, recalled in his memoir that he had "the best seat in the house" that night as leader of a flight of jets sent from the carrier U.S.S. *Ticonderoga* to help defend the destroyers from their supposed attackers. He said he could see the two destroyers' every move vividly, but saw no enemy. "There was absolutely no gunfire except our own, no PT boat wakes, not a candle light let alone a burning ship," he wrote. Stockdale later retired with the rank of admiral, and was Ross Perot's running mate in the 1992 presidential campaign.

Lyndon Johnson's secretary of defense, Robert McNamara,

was one of the last to concede the mistake. In June 1996, he told interviewers for CNN: "I think it is now clear [the second attack] did not occur. I asked [North Vietnamese] General Giap myself, when I visited Hanoi in November of 1995, whether it had occurred, and he said no. I accept that."

Disinformation also accompanied the first U.S. war against Iraq, in 1991. One example is a chilling eyewitness account given by a fifteen-year-old Kuwaiti girl who described the Iraqi troops invading her country as baby-killers. In her widely reported testimony before a body of the U.S. House of Representatives, "Nayirah" said she had been a hospital volunteer when the invasion happened: "I saw the Iraqi soldiers come into the hospital with guns. They took the babies out of the incubators and left the babies to die on the cold floor. It was horrifying."

"Nayirah" 's testimony was endorsed implicitly by Democrat Tom Lantos and Republican John Porter, the chairmen of the Congressional Human Rights Caucus, who sponsored her appearance. They said her last name must be kept secret to prevent reprisals against her family in Kuwait. Furthermore, the independent human rights group Amnesty International produced a report saying that 312 premature infants had died after Iraqi soldiers turned them out of incubators. President George H. W. Bush repeated the baby-killer story again and again. Seven U.S. senators cited it in speeches backing a resolution to go to war with Iraq.

But the story was false. "Nayirah" turned out to be a member of the Kuwaiti royal family, the daughter of the country's ambassador to Washington. She had been fobbed off on the Human Rights Caucus by Hill and Knowlton, a public-relations firm paid by Kuwait to whip up anti-Iraq war fever among Americans. Staffers at the Kuwaiti hospital in "Nayirah" 's story said the things she described hadn't happened. After more investigation, Amnesty International said it "found no reliable evidence that Iraqi forces had caused the deaths of babies by removing them from incubators," and Amnesty withdrew its earlier report.

The truth wasn't revealed until after the United States had expelled Iraq from Kuwait, allowing the ABC reporter John Martin to reach the hospital and interview staff. He broke the news on March 15, 1991, more than five months after "Nayirah" testified. Her identity as the ambassador's daughter wasn't revealed until nearly a year later, in January 1992. By then the war against the "baby killers" was long over.

A Military Duty to Lie

In the case of war, accurate information is especially hard to come by. Military commanders consider it their duty to deceive the enemy if that will win battles and save lives among their own troops. Sometimes that means deceiving the public as well, as in the 1982 Falklands War, when Britain sent a fleet to recapture these South Atlantic islands from Argentina. When an invasion seemed near, Sir Frank Cooper, an under secretary at the British Ministry of Defence, discouraged reporters from thinking there would be a Normandy-style operation with "the landing ships dashing up to the beaches and chaps storming out and lying on their tummies and wriggling up through barbed wire." Relying on that, British reporters told the public that "hit and run" attacks were to be expected, rather than a major battle. Reporters in the United States and elsewhere followed suit, and were badly misled—as were the Argentine defenders. They were taken by surprise the following night when a full-scale amphibious operation commenced at points around an inlet called San Carlos Water on East Falkland Island. The roughly sixty Argentine defenders were overwhelmed, and soon at least 4,000 British troops were ashore. From that secure beachhead, they advanced on the island's major settlements and forced an Argentine surrender less than a month later.

Reporters complained bitterly about the way in which they had been manipulated. Sir Terence Lewin, chief of the British defense staff, responded: "I do not see it as deceiving the press or the public; I see it as deceiving the enemy. What I am trying to do is to win. Anything I can do to help me win is fair as far as I'm concerned, and I would have thought that that was what the Government and the public and the media would want, too, provided the outcome was the one we were all after." That's the way military commanders have seen it since the time of the Greeks and the Trojans. The Chinese general Sun Tzu summed it up 2,500 years ago: "All warfare is based on deception." We doubt that will change any time soon.

It is especially difficult to get the facts right in the chaos and confusion of war, as the Tonkin Gulf incident amply illustrates. The Prussian general Carl von Clausewitz famously observed in 1832 that leaders in battle operate in a kind of feeble twilight like "a fog or moonshine." And because so much military information is classified, the public is in even worse shape when it comes to getting accurate information about war. Often the truth emerges only in histories written a generation or more after the event.

We can't say how history would have turned out had American citizens known the truth about the *Maine,* or the truth about what happened in the Tonkin Gulf, or the truth about the Iraqi "baby killers" in 1991, or the truth about Saddam Hussein's lack of chemical, biological, or nuclear weapons in 2003. In each case the United States had other reasons for war: the desire to grab pieces of Spain's doddering empire in 1898; the wish to evict an aggressor from Kuwait and its oilfields in 1991. Perhaps none of the wars would have been averted. But then again, had the public known the

> ### The Fog of War
>
> ------------------------
>
> The great uncertainty of all data in war is a peculiar difficulty, because all action must, to a certain extent, be planned in a mere twilight, which in addition not infrequently—like the effect of a fog or moonshine—gives to things exaggerated dimensions and unnatural appearance. What this feeble light leaves indistinct to the sight, talent must discover, or must be left to chance.
> —GENERAL CARL VON CLAUSEWITZ, *On War* (1832)

facts, war fever might well have run lower, and leaders might have acted differently. We can never know for sure. What we *do* know is that the Spanish-American War, the Vietnam War, and two Iraq wars were begun, at least in part, under false pretenses.

When war talk runs hot, keep an open mind and keep asking yourself, "I wonder how this will look when the history books are written?"

Fortunately, it's not as hard to get current, accurate information about other matters that bear on our well-being. Even in a world of spin, ordinary citizens can call up reliable sources of information quickly and easily on the Internet. Do you want more information on that miracle prescription medication you saw advertised on television? The full list of side effects is only a few keystrokes away at the Food and Drug Administration's website, and reputable consumer sites contain information about whether it works as well as advertised or is any better than cheaper generic drugs. At www.worstpills.org, for example, you can find strong criticisms of even FDA-approved medications by an aggressive consumer advocate, Dr. Sidney Wolfe. Does that tax-avoidance maneuver you're hearing about seem a bit fishy? The IRS has lots of information about tax scams that it would like to share with you. Has your uncle Bob sent you an e-mail with the subject line "You must read this," which turns out to be a much-forwarded claim that mass marketers are about to run up charges on your cell phone with unwanted sales calls? You can debunk that easily at any of the several websites that specialize in puncturing urban myths, and get authoritative word directly from the Federal Trade Commission itself.

In this chapter, we've been stressing that facts are important. We now turn to how to tell which facts are most important, and how to tell the difference between evidence and random anecdotes. Later on we'll tell you how you can get those facts yourself, using some of the techniques we use every day at FactCheck.org.

Chapter 6

The Great Crow Fallacy

Finding the Best Evidence

TERRY MAPLE WASN'T SURE, BUT HE THOUGHT HE MIGHT HAVE seen a crow using cars to crack walnuts. He had spotted the crow dropping nuts on the pavement one day as he drove through Davis, California. Maple couldn't know that his curious observation would give rise to a twenty-year legend that would significantly elevate crows' status on the avian IQ scale. We tell the story here as a cautionary tale to those with a tendency to draw fast conclusions from limited evidence.

Maple, a psychology professor at the University of California–Davis, published an article in 1974 describing the single crow and its behavior. The title was "Do Crows Use Automobiles as Nutcrackers?" Maple couldn't answer the question, and it wasn't even clear whether the crow he saw had managed to crack the nut it dropped: "I was, unfortunately, unable to return to the scene for a closer look," he wrote. The professor correctly called his observation "an anecdote," meaning an interesting story that suggested crows might use cars to crack walnuts, and that future research might settle the question.

Jump ahead three years, to a November morning in 1977. A biologist named David Grobecker observed a single crow dropping a palm fruit from its beak onto a busy residential street in Long Beach, California. The bird seemed to wait, perched on a lamppost, until a car ran over the fruit and broke it into edible fragments. Then it flew down to eat. This happened twice in the space of about twenty minutes. Grobecker and another biologist, Theodore Pietsch, published an article the following year whose title, "Crows Use Automobiles as Nutcrackers," suggested they had answered the question posed by Maple. "This is indeed an ingenious adjustment to the intrusion of man's technology," the authors concluded.

For nearly twenty years, others cited these two published accounts as evidence of exceptional intelligence in crows. Indeed, some crow fanciers remain convinced—largely on the basis of these two anecdotes—that crows have learned how to use passing cars to crack nuts. But it turns out that although crows are smart birds, they are almost certainly not *that* smart.

How do we know? Because we now have some real data, not single observations or anecdotes. There is a big difference, as the rest of this story illustrates.

The data come from a study published in *The Auk*, the journal of the American Ornithologists' Union, in 1997 by the biologist Daniel Cristol and three colleagues from the University of California. Cristol's study was based on more than a couple of random observations. He and his colleagues watched crows foraging for walnuts on the streets of Davis for a total of over twenty-five hours spread over fourteen days. Just as they had expected, they saw plenty of crows dropping walnuts on the street. Crows, seagulls, and some other birds often drop food onto hard surfaces to crack it open. An estimated 10,000 crows were roosting nearby, and 150 walnut trees lined the streets where the study was conducted. But did the crows deliberately drop walnuts in the path of oncoming cars? The scientists watched how the crows behaved when cars were approaching; then, soon after, they watched how crows behaved at the same places when cars were not approaching, during an equivalent time period.

What they found, after 400 separate observations, was that there was no real difference. In fact, crows were just slightly more likely to drop a walnut on the pavement when no car was approaching. The birds also were slightly more likely to fly away and leave a nut on the pavement in the absence of a car, contrary to what would be expected if the birds really expected cars to crack the nuts for them. Furthermore, the scientists noted that they frequently saw crows dropping walnuts on rooftops, on sidewalks, and in vacant parking lots, where there was no possibility of a car coming along. Not once during the study did a car crack even a single walnut dropped by a crow.

The authors concluded, reasonably enough: "Our observations suggest that crows merely are using the hard road surface to facilitate opening walnuts, and their interactions with cars are incidental." The title of their article: "Crows Do Not Use Automobiles as Nutcrackers: Putting an Anecdote to the Test." The anecdote flunked.

LESSON: *Don't Confuse Anecdotes with Data*

ONE OF OUR FAVORITE SAYINGS—VARIOUSLY ATTRIBUTED TO DIFferent economists—is "The plural of 'anecdote' is not 'data.'" That means simply this: one or two interesting stories don't prove anything. They could be far from typical. In this case, it's fun to think that crows might be clever enough to learn such a neat trick as using human drivers to prepare their meals for them. It's also easy to see how spotting a few crows getting lucky can encourage even serious scientists to think the behavior might be deliberate. But we have to consider the term "anecdotal evidence" as something close to an oxymoron, a contradiction in terms.

Now, it's true that the crow debate continues. Millions of people saw a PBS documentary by David Attenborough that showed Japanese crows putting walnuts in a crosswalk and then returning to eat after passing cars had cracked them. That scene was inspired by an article in the *Japanese Journal of Ornithology* by a psychologist at Tohoku University. But the Japanese article wasn't based on a scientific study; it merely reported more anecdotes: "Because the [crows'] behavior was so sporadic, most observation was made when the author came across the behavior coincidentally on his commute to the campus." That was two years before Cristol and his colleagues finally published their truly systematic study. So for us, the notion that crows deliberately use cars as nutcrackers has been debunked, until and unless better evidence comes along. Even Theodore Pietsch, who coauthored the 1978 article that said crows do use cars as nutcrackers, has changed his view. "When Grobecker and I wrote that paper so long ago, we did it on a whim, took about an hour to write it, and we were shocked that it was accepted for publication almost immediately, with no criticism at all from outside referees," he told us. "I would definitely put much more credibility in a study supported by data rather than random observation." So do we, and so should all of us.

Seeing versus Believing

Avoiding spin and getting a solid grip on hard facts requires not only an open mind and a willingness to consider all the evidence, it requires us to have some basic skills in telling good evidence from bad, and to recognize that mere assertion is not fact and that not all facts are good evidence. As counterintuitive as it may seem, the most basic lesson is that our own personal experience isn't necessarily very good evidence. It's natural to trust what we can see with our own eyes, what we can touch with our own hands and hear with our own ears. But our own experience can mislead us.

LESSON:	*Remember the Blind Men and the Elephant*

IT IS A NATURAL HUMAN TENDENCY TO GIVE GREAT WEIGHT TO OUR immediate experience, as the ancient fable of the blind men and the elephant should remind us. In the version written by the nineteenth-century American poet John Godfrey Saxe, six blind men feel different parts of the elephant and conclude variously that it is like a snake, a wall, a tree, a fan, a spear, or a rope. Then they argue. Saxe's poem concludes:

> And so these men of Indostan, disputed loud and long,
> each in his own opinion, exceeding stiff and strong,
> Though each was partly in the right, and all were in the wrong!

> So, oft in theologic wars, the disputants, I ween,
> tread on in utter ignorance of what each other mean,
> and prate about the elephant not one of them has seen!

Unless we want to "tread on in utter ignorance," like the blind men debating about the elephant, we need to bear in mind that our personal experience seldom gives us a full picture. This is especially true when our experience is indirect, filtered by others.

Consider what happened during the Gulf War of 1991. During the forty-three-day air campaign, television viewers at home watched "smart bombs" homing in unerringly on their targets time after time. A nation that had lost more than 58,000 members of its armed forces in Vietnam a generation earlier now seemed able to fight a new kind of war, from the air, putting hardly any soldiers at risk.

Not surprisingly, military briefers were showing the public only their apparent successes, but no amount of skeptical questioning by reporters could undo the enormous impact of what viewers were seeing on their TV screens. Only long after the war did we learn that a lot of "smart" weapons missed their targets and that just

8 percent of the munitions dropped (measured by tonnage) were guided. Contrary to the picture presented on television, nine of ten bombs dropped were old-fashioned "dumb" ones. This was documented in a 1996 report by the General Accounting Office (which has since been renamed the Government Accountability Office). It wasn't until a decade after the 1991 war that weapons precision actually improved enough to match the false impression created by the selective use of video during Desert Storm. The lesson here is that sometimes what you don't know or haven't been told is *more* important than what you have seen with your own eyes. We humans have a natural tendency to overgeneralize from vivid examples.

The reason we should trust the GAO's report over the evidence offered by our own eyes is that the GAO had access to all the relevant data, including the Pentagon's bomb-damage assessment reports, and it systematically weighed and studied that mass of information. Also, the GAO is an arm of Congress with a reputation for even-handed evaluation and for casting a skeptical eye on the claims of agencies (such as the Pentagon) that seek taxpayer money for their programs. The GAO study relied on evidence; what Pentagon briefers showed Americans during the war was a collection of anecdotes—and carefully selected anecdotes at that. The public saw few if any "smart" bombs miss, when in fact they missed much of the time. War was made to seem less messy, less morally objectionable, than it really is.

The Great Fertilizer Scare

Without real data and hard evidence, it's easy to be led astray in all sorts of matters, especially when a dramatic story involving well-known figures captures our attention. The Great Fertilizer Scare of 1987 will illustrate. It began when a former San Francisco 49ers quarterback, Bob Waters, was diagnosed with amyotrophic lateral sclerosis, also known as Lou Gehrig's disease, and it was reported that two other players from the 1964 team also had ALS. Soon newspapers were carrying a story saying a common lawn fertilizer, Milorganite, which a groundskeeper recalled using on the 49ers practice field, was suspected as a cause.

Milorganite is sewage sludge, recycled by the Milwaukee Metropolitan Sewerage District. It is dried for forty minutes at between 840 and 1,200 degrees Fahrenheit, a process that kills bacteria and viruses, but it does contain tiny amounts of certain elements, including cadmium, which some researchers at the time suspected might be a cause of the disease. A Milwaukee newspaper dug up the fact that two former Milorganite plant workers also had died of ALS (out of 155 total deaths among workers, from all causes) and that 25 ALS patients in the Milwaukee area claimed to have been in contact with Milorganite. *Time* magazine and The Associated Press, among others, also ran stories citing a "possible" link between Milorganite and ALS.

But tragic as slow death from ALS certainly is, the story of the three celebrity football players is a bit like our tale of the great crow fallacy. An EPA epidemiologist who headed a team to study the matter, Patricia A. Murphy, said the ALS-Milorganite connection "has been blown up out of some groundskeeper's imagination." She found no evidence of an increase in ALS in the Milwaukee area or Wisconsin as a whole, and concluded that "the anecdotal stories linking ALS and Milorganite are purely that, i.e., anecdotal with no basis in scientific fact." Dr. Henry Anderson, Wisconsin's state environmental epidemiologist, agreed. He reported that scientific evidence against Milorganite was lacking and recommended that the state not give high priority to further study. The three 49ers might not even have been exposed to Milorganite. No records were ever found to support the groundskeeper's recollection. Even if the three players had been exposed to Milorganite, they appear to constitute what statisticians call a random cluster, meaning an unusually large grouping that occurs purely by chance. Epidemiologists are trained to look at the whole picture without being misled by such coincidental clusters. Sooner or later, if you toss a coin enough times, it will come up heads ten times in a row. The odds of it coming up heads on any given toss, however, are always 50–50. And the odds that Milorganite had anything to do with ALS are somewhere between very low and zero.

Mitch Snyder's "Meaningless" Numbers

Real evidence, unlike attention-grabbing anecdotes, is generated by systematic study. But not all studies are created equal, and some hardly deserve to be called studies at all. Consider a claim made in 1982 that more than 3 million Americans could be homeless. It was widely reported as an estimate that 3 million *were* homeless, and it was widely believed. Critics of the Reagan administration saw the figure as evidence that the Republican president's policies were creating a social calamity on a scale not seen since the days of the Dust Bowl and the Great Depression. Had 3 million been an accurate number, it would have meant that one American in every seventy-seven was living on the street.

In fact, the figure was close to an outright fabrication. The source was Mitch Snyder, a former advertising man and ex-convict (he served a federal prison term for grand theft, auto) who had turned himself into an advocate for the homeless and an unrelenting detractor of Ronald Reagan. His methods were hardly scientific. In 1980, he and others at the Community for Creative Non-Violence had called up one hundred local clergy, city officials, and others involved in aiding the homeless in twenty-five cities, asking them for a quick estimate of the number of homeless persons in their locality. But an estimate is not a count, and some estimates are more reliable than others. For one thing, CCNV rejected estimates that Snyder deemed too low. On this highly subjective basis, the group concluded that one percent of the entire U.S. population, or about 2.2 million people, were homeless at the time of the survey. Then, after a recession hit the economy, CCNV said, "We are convinced the number of homeless people in the United States could reach

3 million or more in 1983." But that was nothing more than their guess piled on top of a dubious "average" of their cherry-picked estimates.

While testifying before the House Subcommittee on Housing on May 24, 1984, Snyder was challenged to support his estimate; he all but admitted that he had pulled the number from thin air. He said: "These numbers are in fact meaningless. We have tried to satisfy your gnawing curiosity for a number because we are Americans with western little minds that have to quantify everything in sight, whether we can or not." But few reporters took note; instead, many repeated the "meaningless" 3 million estimate for years without conveying any sense of its spurious basis. More than seven years after Snyder confessed that his number was "meaningless," for example, the CBS reporter John Roberts stated flatly that there were "more than three million homeless in America."

LESSON: *Not All "Studies" Are Equal*

SOME QUESTIONS TO ASK WHEN THINKING ABOUT A DRAMATIC FACTUAL claim:

- Who stands behind the information?

- Does the source have an ax to grind?

- What method did the source use to obtain the information?

- How old are the data?

- What assumptions did those collecting the information make?

- How much guesswork was involved?

Today, we can say with some confidence that homeless people in the United States number in the hundreds of thousands, not in the millions. This is still a lot of people without a home, but it's a fraction of what Snyder claimed.

In late March 2000, the U.S. Census Bureau *counted* 170,706 persons in homeless shelters and soup lines and at a number of open-air locations, such as under the Brooklyn Bridge, where homeless persons were known to gather. The Census Bureau says that figure shouldn't be taken as a count of all the homeless—it concedes, for example, that it missed anyone who was not using a shelter on that early spring day, or who was sleeping in an open-air location other than those checked. But at least we can be certain that those 170,706 homeless persons were actually counted.

How many were missed is still open to question. Martha Burt, an expert at the Urban Institute who has studied homelessness for years, estimates that homeless people number no fewer than 444,000 and that the figure is probably closer to 842,000. Her estimates are projections based on an unprecedented, onetime Census Bureau survey of thousands of programs providing services to the homeless in seventy-six cities, suburbs, and rural areas. In October and November 1996, the bureau counted the persons being served at a random sample of those service locations and interviewed a random sampling of 4,207 clients to get additional information. The survey wasn't intended or designed to produce a national estimate of the homeless population, and the Census Bureau didn't attempt to derive one. But Burt made a few assumptions and calculated that nationally the number would have been 444,000 homeless adults and children using services on an average week in October and November, the months in which the Census Bureau conducted its head count. Burt also estimated that 842,000 homeless adults and children would have used services nationally on an average week in February, when the weather is much colder. Her estimates are just that—estimates—but they extrapolate from solid data, on the basis of assumptions that are fully disclosed.

Something else gives us confidence in Burt's estimate that between 444,000 and 842,000 Americans are homeless: several other studies using different but still systematic methods have come up with figures that are generally in the same range. When different methods arrive at similar estimates, those estimates are more credible. We call this "convergent evidence."

A Taxing Argument

As a general rule, the source of evidence matters. Snyder's figures should have been viewed with a critical eye from the start both because he was lobbying for more federal spending to aid homeless people and because he was a bitter critic of the Reagan administration. While there are certainly scrupulously honest advocates out there, it's clear that Snyder's figures were "data in the service of ideology." But we can place more trust in studies and data from sources that have no horse in the race, and who haven't deceived us in the past. Such sources often give us a picture very different from the one painted by self-interested people who are trying to sell us something, whether it's a product or a policy.* Examine, for example, the dubious charges made against the federal estate tax by the lobbyists and partisans who sought its repeal.

"Death Tax" Bunk

RADIO AD:

When you die, the IRS can bury your family in crippling tax bills. It can cost them everything. What's worse, the death tax is a double tax on all you've worked to build.

(American Family Business Institute, June 2005)

PRESIDENT GEORGE W. BUSH:

We also put the death tax on the road to extinction because farmers and small business owners should not be taxed twice after a lifetime of work.

(Radio address, January 21, 2006)

---

* There's a scholarly argument to be made that everybody has some sort of bias, and therefore there's no possibility of a neutral viewpoint. In a philosophical sense that may well be so, but it's not relevant here. As a practical matter we find we're more likely to get trustworthy information from disinterested sources than from advocates.

Farmers and small businesses were under attack in the year 2005, if a radio ad from that year is to be believed: "When you die, the IRS can bury your family in crippling tax bills. It can cost them everything." That claim was in a radio ad that ran in eight states in 2005, part of what the sponsor said was a $15 million campaign to repeal the tax permanently. The ad was paid for by the American Family Business Institute, a group made up of about 500 businesses and including three billionaires, according to organizers. Others known to have funded anti-estate-tax lobbying include the billionaire Mars candy and Gallo wine clans.

The same claim had been picked up by the Republican party and had become part of its antitax orthodoxy. President Bush repeated it throughout his tenure of office, saying six weeks after his inauguration that Congress should "eliminate the death tax so family farmers aren't forced to sell their farms before they want to." But the notion that farmers are forced to sell out and that families can lose "everything" is simply false.

The fact is, as the nonpartisan Congressional Budget Office said in a report issued in July 2005: "The vast majority of estates, including those of farmers and small-business owners, had enough liquid assets to pay the estate taxes they owed." In other words, the "vast majority" had no need to sell any assets at all—let alone "everything"—to pay estate taxes. The CBO said that returns filed in 2000 showed only 138 farmers and 164 family business owners left estates without enough liquid assets to pay their estate taxes. And the CBO estimated that those numbers would fall to fifteen farmers and sixty-two family business owners by the year 2006, when only estates valued at $2 million or more would be subject to any tax.

The CBO was putting matters cautiously. *The New York Times* reported in 2001 that one of the leading advocates for estate tax repeal, the American Farm Bureau, "said it could not cite a single example of a farm lost because of estate taxes." The Farm Bureau, a huge lobbying organization that calls itself "the voice of agriculture," then went scrambling to find such an example. Within days of the *Times* report, the organization's president issued an internal bulletin saying: "It is crucial for us to be able to provide Congress with examples of farmers and ranchers who have lost farms or have had to sell off portions of their land that makes [sic] the remaining parcel 'inefficient,' due to death taxes." The memo was quoted by *Congressional Quarterly Daily Monitor,* which also said no examples had been found. When we called the Farm Bureau in early 2006, they weren't very happy to hear from us, and they still could not point to a farm lost to pay estate taxes.

That anyone could "lose everything" to the estate tax is a logical impossibility, anyway. As of 2006, there is no tax at all on the first $2 million of any estate (effectively, $4 million for a couple that takes certain estate planning steps). The maximum tax rate is 46 percent (and set to go down to 45 percent in 2007) on anything above those amounts. Far from losing everything, heirs keep most.

We're not arguing for or against estate taxes. We are saying that hard data from tax returns, analyzed by a nonpartisan body noted for its consistent use of reliable methods, show that one of the principal claims made against the estate tax is false. There's another argument, with which economists generally agree, that taxing wealth reduces the incentive to invest and in turn holds back economic growth and job creation. That argument isn't very popular with the public, but at least it's honest. We can't say that about the radio ad warning that "your family" could be "buried" by the tax. In fact, the estate tax fell upon only 1.17 percent of the estates of adults who died in 2002, according to the IRS Statistics of Income. In other words, nearly 99 percent of the people who heard those radio ads wouldn't be touched by the tax at all. With respect to them, the ads were flatly untrue.

LESSON: *Saying It Doesn't Make It So*

CRITICS OF THE ESTATE TAX BASED THEIR YEARS-LONG CAMPAIGN on the idea that repealing the tax would primarily benefit farmers and small-business owners. But most of the wealthy few who pay the tax aren't farmers or small-business owners by any definition. And the vast majority of small-business owners and farmers will never pay a penny of estate tax. Constant repetition of the claim may have caused people to believe it, but repetition didn't make it true.

An Abortion Distortion

Bogus studies pop up in politics all the time. In 2005, Democrats were gloating over a macabre statistic that would have embarrassed President Bush, if it had been true. They said the number of abortions had gone up since this anti-abortion president took office, and they blamed his economic policies for driving poor women to end pregnancies rather than bear children whom they would be unable to support. Citing "the draconian policies" of Republicans, John Kerry proclaimed, "And do you know that in fact abortion has gone up in these last few years?" The Democratic National Committee chairman, Howard Dean, even went so far as to quantify the purported increase during an appearance on NBC News's *Meet the Press:* "You know that abortions have gone up 25 percent since George Bush was president?" In fact, the respected Guttmacher Institute, whose figures on abortion trends are systematically gathered using a disclosed method and are used by both sides—reported that the number of abortions performed in the United States had continued its twenty-year decline after Bush took office. According to the institute's most recent figures, published in 2006, abortions declined in each of the first three years of Bush's tenure, for a total drop of nearly 2 percent.

The false claim that abortions were rising originated with a flawed "study" by Glen Harold Stassen, who is neither a statistician nor a healthcare expert, but an ethics professor at Fuller Theological Seminary. Stassen's article originally appeared not in any scientific journal but in a liberal Christian publication, *Sojourners,* in October 2004. "Under President Bush, the decade-long trend of declining abortion rates appears to have reversed," he wrote. "Given the trends of the 1990s, 52,000 more abortions occurred in the United States in 2002 than would have been expected before this change of direction." Stassen cited data from sixteen states. The claim was picked up and repeated uncritically on many Internet web logs, both liberal and conservative, and by Democrats including Kerry and Dean.

> **LESSON:** *Extraordinary Claims Need Extraordinary Evidence*

AS THIS TABLE ILLUSTRATES, THE DRAMATIC CLAIM THAT ABORTIONS had suddenly begun to increase—after twenty years of almost uninterrupted annual decreases—begged for confirmation.

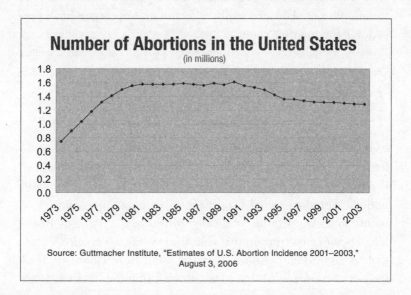

Number of Abortions in the United States
(in millions)

Source: Guttmacher Institute, "Estimates of U.S. Abortion Incidence 2001–2003," August 3, 2006

Before accepting any such claims, it is wise to first look carefully at the source. In this case, the claim that the trend had suddenly reversed came from a critic of Republican policies who had no track record of evaluating abortion statistics and no special expertise in the field; in addition, the claim was based on fragmentary information.

Stassen got the data wrong for two reasons. First, he tried to project a national trend from an unscientific, nonrandom sample. He used the first sixteen states to report their official abortion data to the federal Centers for Disease Control, without waiting for the other thirty-four states to report. That's like trying to predict the outcome of a presidential election after the first sixteen states close their polls and report their results. Second, in two of the states among Stassen's sixteen, the Guttmacher Institute found the reporting system unreliable. In Colorado, where Stassen claimed that rates "skyrocketed 111 percent," the reporting procedure had been changed in order to compensate for historic underreporting. What Stassen thought was an increase in the number of abortions really reflected an improvement in procedures for counting them.

CASE STUDY: *Is Cold-Eeze "Clinically Proven?"*

EVEN A GOOD STUDY FROM A REPUTABLE SOURCE CAN BE MISLEADING, if the results can't be replicated. If you've ever gotten the sniffles and shopped for a drugstore cold remedy, you've probably noticed a product called Cold-Eeze, which contains a zinc compound and claims to be "clinically proven to cut colds by nearly half." Science has proven this zinc stuff works! Or has it? A close look at the evidence shows that the Cold-Eeze claim—indeed, the entire company—is based largely on a single study from 1996.

But several other studies have produced starkly different results.

The original study, still cited on the Cold-Eeze website as we write this, was done at the Cleveland Clinic Foundation by Dr. Michael Macknin. That study and Macknin's many subsequent news interviews sent Cold-Eeze flying off drugstore shelves. He told Barbara Walters on ABC's 20/20 in January 1997 that he "got goose bumps" when he tabulated the data, and added, "here was something that actually seemed like it was helping the common cold, and nothing had really worked like this before." The price of stock in the Quigley Corporation, which sells Cold-Eeze, soared, going from about $2 a share before the study was published to a high of $37 at the time of the 20/20 broadcast.

The first study seemed solid enough. It was published in a reputable, peer-reviewed journal, *Annals of Internal Medicine*. And it was a double-blind study: forty-nine subjects got the Cold-Eeze lozenges, fifty got a placebo, and neither the subjects nor the persons dispensing the lozenges knew which was which until the time came to tally the results. But when Macknin conducted a second study, of 249 suburban Cleveland students in grades one through twelve, he found that the kids who received the placebo got over colds just as quickly as those getting Cold-Eeze. The lozenges "were not effective in treating cold symptoms in children and adolescents," said the report, published in *The Journal of the American Medical Association* in June 1998. It added that further research was needed "to clarify what role, if any, zinc may play in treating cold symptoms." Quigley's stock plunged. The company had actually paid for Macknin's second study, but it doesn't display that one on its website.

Since that 1996 study that launched Cold-Eeze sales, the evidence has continued to be mixed. Over the years some scientific studies have found that zinc gluconate (the featured ingredient of Cold-Eeze) seemed to reduce the duration and severity of cold symptoms, but several other scientific studies have found no such effect. The National Institutes of Health have concluded: "Additional research is needed to determine whether zinc compounds have any effect on the common cold." Zinc might work, or it might not.

So Cold-Eeze turns out to be another brand built on spin, like Listerine. In 1999, the Federal Trade Commission accused Quigley of false advertising for claiming on the QVC shopping network that its lozenges could actually *prevent* colds. The FTC said Quigley had no reasonable evidence to support such claims, and Quigley settled the case by agreeing to stop making them. Also false, in our view, is the company's biggest selling point, its claim that Cold-Eeze is "clinically proven" to cut cold symptoms by 42 percent. The best the company can say truthfully is that Cold-Eeze has been clinically *tested*, with inconclusive results.

Non-Evidence: Linus Pauling and Bruce Willis

We've shown that anecdotes can mislead us, and that sloppy, biased, or made-up studies can masquerade as evidence, and that even good studies can fail to hold up when set beside later research. Here are a few other things that do not count as evidence.

APPEALS TO AUTHORITY   Linus Pauling won two Nobel Prizes, one for chemistry and the other for peace, but he had no particular expertise in medicine. Nevertheless, millions of people swallowed his claims that high doses of vitamin C could cut the incidence of the common cold and might even be effective against cancer. In fact, at least sixteen controlled experiments, some involving thousands of volunteers, have failed to show that vitamin C has any effect on either condition. Dr. Stephen Barrett of Quackwatch.org reports that "no responsible medical or nutrition scientists share [Pauling's] views."

FactCheck.org's Guide to Testing Evidence

At FactCheck.org, we find ourselves asking a few basic questions again and again in evaluating evidence. Here's a short list of tests we have found useful:

- Is the source highly regarded and widely accepted? There are a number of long-standing organizations we know we can count on for reliable, unbiased information. For job statistics, the Bureau of Labor Statistics is every economist's basic source. For hurricane statistics, the National Hurricane Center is considered the authority. For determining when business recessions begin and end, the private, nonprofit National Bureau of Economic Research is an authority cited in economic history books. And for abortion statistics, the Guttmacher Institute is accepted by all sides as trustworthy.

- Is the source an advocate? Claims made by political parties, candidates, lobbying groups, salesmen, and other advocates may be true but are usually self-serving and as a result may be misleading; they require special scrutiny. Always compare their information with other sources. The National Research Council—chartered by Congress and able to call on the nation's most eminent experts—is a better source on whether gun-control laws cut crime than is a group devoted to lobbying for or against such laws. The Guttmacher Institute does advocate "reproductive freedom," but we accept its numbers not only because the institute is trusted by both sides of the debate, but also because in this case they support a president who is on the other side of the issue. The institute's report that the number of abortions continues to diminish under Bush is the opposite of what we would expect if it were allowing ideological bias to color its findings.

- What is the source's track record? Look for previous experience. In our abortion example, Stassen had no record of conducting studies on abortion statistics. In contrast, the Guttmacher Institute's surveys of abortion providers go back to 1973.

- What method is used? Mitch Snyder's estimate of the number of homeless people turned out to depend on a collection of guesses, at best. The Urban Institute's estimates, though they also involve some assumptions and guesswork, are based on U.S. Census data gathered in a uniform way from a very large, random sample.

- Does the source "show its work"? Good researchers always explain how they arrived at their numbers and conclusions. Daniel Cristol described exactly how he and his colleagues conducted their 400 timed observations of crows, and he published the results. Good research methods are transparent.

- Is the sample random? News organizations and websites are fond of conducting "unscientific" polls. Viewers or visitors are asked to express a preference, and the results are reported. This is just a marketing method designed to draw interest; the results are utterly meaningless because the sample is self-selected, not random. Some such polls have even been intentionally rigged. At best, they are like Stassen's nonrandom sixteen-state sample, which turned out not to reflect the situation in all fifty states.

- Is there a control group? Good scientific procedure requires a "control" to provide a valid basis for comparison. A crow dropping nuts in front of a car proves nothing. Cristol watched crows when cars were coming, but he also watched crows when cars were *not* coming, and he observed the difference (none). In tests of new drugs one group gets a placebo, with no active ingredients, to provide a point of comparison with the group that gets the actual drug.

- Does the source have the requisite skill? A trained epidemiologist should be trusted more than a newspaper headline writer to evaluate whether a cluster of cancer cases was caused by something in the water, or was just a statistical fluke.

- Have the results been replicated, or contradicted? Sometimes one study tells a story that isn't backed up by later research. Have the results been repeated in similar studies? Do other researchers agree, or do they come up with contrary findings? The Cold-Eeze story shows how cherry-picked studies can mislead us.

The lesson here is that somebody who is an authority in one field isn't necessarily qualified in another. Sam Waterston plays a smart, tough prosecutor on television's *Law & Order* series, but so far as we know he has no special expertise as a financial adviser. So why should we give any special weight to his TV commercials praising the brokerage firm TD Waterhouse? Bruce Willis endorsed President George H. W. Bush in 1992 and supported the current war in Iraq, but his portrayal of action heroes on the screen is no reason to give his political or military views any more weight than your next-door neighbor's. The same goes for Martin Sheen's endorsement of Howard Dean in the 2004 Democratic presidential primary. Playing a president on TV is about as valid a qualification for making political judgments as playing a doctor on TV might be in recommending decaffeinated coffee, the way Robert Young did in the 1970s, after starring in *Marcus Welby, MD* on television.

Before relying on any authority, ask yourself, "Is this source competent? Does he know what he's talking about? Does she have any real evidence? Do other authorities in the same field agree?"

| APPEALS TO POPULARITY | Advertisers use these all the time. A typical ex-ample: a hospital in Saginaw, Michigan, says it |

is "preferred two to one." Does having a large number of patients mean that a hospital provides the best care? Not necessarily. It might simply have better parking or be located more conveniently.

Other examples to look out for: "top-selling"; "number one"; "preferred over . . ." In politics the "front runner" is often the candidate to watch, but is not necessarily the best one or even the one destined to win, as onetime front runner Howard Dean discovered in the 2004 Democratic primary races. And in February 2006, both Ford and General Motors were claiming to be the top-selling brand of automobiles in the United States, as figures on 2005 vehicle registrations trickled in. In fact, both automakers had been losing ground for years, falling from a combined 60 percent of the U.S. market in 1986 to about 45 percent in 2005. Each might just as easily have said it was "preferred by fewer and fewer."

Popularity may settle elections, but it doesn't settle questions of fact. Ask yourself, "Is this thing popular because it's good, or for some other reason, such as a big advertising budget?"

| FAULTY |
| LOGIC |

Whole books and several websites have been devoted to the question of logical fallacies. One that
trips up many people is the idea that when two events happen, the
first one has caused the second. In Latin, this is called the *post hoc,
ergo propter hoc* fallacy, meaning "after this, therefore because of
this."

The *post hoc* fallacy is seductive because of what we observe to
be true in our daily lives. We step on the car's accelerator; the car
moves forward. We flip on a light switch; the light comes on. We
touch a lit match to kindling; the kindling catches fire. We may be
disappointed, however, if we assume that the shirt we put on before
a successful fishing trip is therefore a "lucky" shirt that will magi-
cally produce fish the next time. That's just superstition. When we
fall prey to the *post hoc* fallacy, we're like the rooster who thought
his crowing made the sun rise.

Consider a statement being made in early 2006 by the Brady
Campaign, formerly known as Handgun Control, Inc. The campaign stated that passage of the Brady Law in 1993 (imposing
background checks for handgun purchasers) and the federal "assault weapons" ban in 1994 (which banned the sale of certain
semi-automatic weapons) were followed by years of declines in
violent crime. This the group cited as proof that "gun laws work."

It's true that crime rates plunged throughout the 1990s, starting just about the time the two gun laws were enacted. But that
doesn't mean that the gun laws *caused* the decline. Criminologists,
economists, and just about everybody else are still debating over
what did. Proposed causes include increased numbers of police,
the practice of "community policing," "zero-tolerance" policies, and
even the legalization of abortion two decades earlier. In late 2004,
the Committee on Law and Justice of the National Research Council examined the question whether gun laws affect crime rates, and
concluded that a connection couldn't be shown: "In summary, the
committee concludes that existing research studies and data . . . do
not credibly demonstrate a causal relationship between the owner-

ship of firearms and the causes or prevention of criminal violence or suicide."

Be careful about jumping to conclusions. Always ask, "Are these facts really connected?"

And—always—keep asking, "What's the evidence?"

ALWAYS CHECK the FOOTNOTES!
INFORMATION IS NOT KNOWLEDGE.*
A. EINSTEIN
*I NEVER SAID THIS!
SIGHE

Chapter 7

Osama, Ollie, and Al

The Internet Solution

SO FAR WE'VE POINTED OUT HOW TO RECOGNIZE SPIN AND MISINFOR-mation, explained some of the tricks that spinners use to mislead us, and described the psychological traps that too often make us ac-complices in our own deception. We've said that staying unspun can save us money, embarrassment, and perhaps even our lives, but that it also requires us to adjust our mental habits so that we look actively for facts that might *disprove* whatever we happen to believe at the moment, rather than giving in to our hardwired human ten-dency to see only supporting evidence. And we've discussed the ba-sics of how to tell good evidence from random anecdotes. Now it's time to talk about where, and how, to find the solid facts you need.

The solution to spin is the Internet, if you use it very carefully. *The Wall Street Journal*'s personal-technology columnist, Walt Mossberg, may have put it best: "The World Wide Web is a mar-velous thing. Because it exists, more people have direct access to more knowledge than at any time in history." That's true—and there's more reliable information being added every day. Furthermore, much of this information is available to everyone, for only the price of an Internet connection.

Unfortunately, as you probably know, the Web is also a conduit for new gushers of toxic informational sludge as well. Anybody can say anything they want on the Internet, regardless of whether it is true, and people can post anonymously or under a false identity. We've already mentioned websites that tout fraudulent products, and con artists who use mass e-mailings to reach their victims. The trick is to sort the gold from the dross. We'll show you how to do that, and perhaps even have some fun along the way.

To illustrate, we offer the story of an Internet hoax that was swallowed by untold thousands of gullible believers—and we show how to find the facts.

Osama, Ollie, and Al

Within weeks after the calamity of September 11, 2001, an e-mail began to circulate containing what the anonymous author described as "stunning" information. He (or she) claimed that Oliver North had warned Congress as far back as 1987 that Osama bin Laden is "the most evil man alive" and had said, "I would recommend that an assassin team be formed to eliminate him and his men from the face of the earth." Furthermore, this message stated, the senator questioning North was Albert Gore of Tennessee, the future vice president and Democratic candidate for president.

This message was red meat to a lot of conservatives. At a time when President Bush was being criticized for ignoring warnings of a possible terrorist attack, the idea that Al Gore could have prevented 9/11 if only he had listened to a former Ronald Reagan aide was irresistible. The message was forwarded and reforwarded countless times.

The message referred to North's televised testimony before a

Senate committee investigating the Iran-Contra affair. North, now a conservative political commentator, was then a lieutenant colonel in the U.S. Marine Corps and had played a key role in the scandal as a White House military aide involved in secretly aiding the Contra rebels of Nicaragua in their attempt to overthrow the leftist president of Nicaragua, Daniel Ortega. But the message was totally false. In 1987, bin Laden was in Afghanistan fighting the Soviet Union, not the United States. He didn't form al Qaeda until the following year. Gore didn't question North: he wasn't even a member of the Iran-Contra investigating committee. The man questioning North was John Nields, the investigating committee's lawyer. The security system cost $13,800 (according to North's subsequent indictment) and not $60,000.

Yet this nonsense still circulates. Our inbox at FactCheck.org contains messages from dozens of people who have received the hoax, asking us whether there is anything to it. A woman who said she lives just blocks from the site of the World Trade Center called us in January 2006 after her brother sent her a version of the message complete with color photos of the Twin Towers burning. She said that despite her expressions of skepticism, her brother insisted it was true. There were plenty of reasons for the sister to question the message. Why isn't North himself hammering away at it constantly on Fox News, where he is host of a weekly program? Would Al Gore really have asked softball questions such as "Why are you so afraid of this man?" at a nationally televised hearing?

The brother swallowed this bunkum, we suspect, because he wanted to believe it. The Ollie-Osama-Al fairy tale made liberal Democrats look like fools and the hard-nosed conservative North look like a prophet. It also shifted blame for the failure to foresee the 9/11 attacks away from incumbent President George W. Bush. While we can't read the brother's mind, he probably fell into the "root for my side" trap we described in Chapter 4. What's certain is that he failed to adopt the active open-mindedness that could have saved him from being fooled. We know this because he not only failed to note the warning signs that made his sister doubt this tale, he also failed to make even a feeble effort to look for contrary evidence. And he could have found that evidence with no more effort than it took him to forward the fable to his sister.

What Ollie Really Said

As we write this, an Internet search for the keywords "Oliver North" plus "bin Laden" brings up literally dozens of articles disputing the hoax. That would have told our correspondent's brother that, at the very least, there were serious doubts about the accuracy of the story, and that a little more research was called for. The very first hit on our search was an article headlined "Oliver Twisted," which flatly declares that the story of the hearing is false.

Why should we believe this article and not an e-mail message, which may have come from a trusted friend or relative? Actually, we shouldn't believe either of them, not automatically. So far we've discovered only that the e-mail *may* be a hoax and that we need to dig more deeply.

First, we evaluate the "Oliver Twisted" article. It gives the sources of its information in footnotes, thus enabling us to check what's being said. Also, the article appears on Snopes.com, a website that has been around for years and is run by two California folklore experts, Barbara and David P. Mikkelson, who are devoted to examining the many urban legends that have migrated to the Web. That's another point in favor of Snopes.com, a site that isn't pushing any particular political agenda or point of view. As we look farther down our search list, we also find that half a dozen similar websites, all of them devoted to debunking false Internet rumors, are also calling the Ollie-Osama-Al story false. So far, the neutral bunk-busters are unanimous: this is a scam.

And the final proof is also right there on the Internet. Midway down the first page of our search results, we find a link to the U.S. Senate, which has devoted a brief article to exposing this very hoax.

Better yet, the Senate staff has posted a copy of the actual tran-
script of the 1987 hearings into the Iran-Contra affair at which
North gave his testimony. Gore wasn't there. Committee lawyer
Nields did the questioning. North named Abu Nidal, not bin Laden.
Case closed. (If you want to see the transcript yourself, go to www.
senate.gov/reference/resources/pdf/ollie.pdf.)

Incidentally, North himself has tried to set the record straight
a number of times. On his own website (www.olivernorth.com), he
writes that he has received "several thousand e-mails from every
state in the U.S. and 13 foreign countries" asking about the bin
Laden hoax message, which he called "simply inaccurate."

Finding the Good Stuff

We could cite countless examples here of false information floating
around the Internet; you probably have seen plenty as well. The Internet is pure anarchy: more information is available more readily
than ever before, but there are no regulations, no standards, and no
penalties for making careless mistakes or even for telling the most
outrageous conceivable whoppers. Fortunately, finding the good
stuff can be fairly easy, and even fun. We've already demonstrated
how quickly the Oliver North hoax could be shot down. The key is
finding the right websites and knowing how to evaluate their reli-
ability. In the remainder of this chapter, we'll share with you a few
of the things we've learned at FactCheck.org about finding trustworthy information on the Web.

First and most important, consider the source. Who stands
behind the information? The Ollie North hoax was anonymous, impossible to trace back to the person who originated it. The author
claimed to have seen a videotape of North "at a lecture the other
day," which of course is also impossible to verify. Claims from such
sources deserve no credence whatever because you have no idea
who is making the claim, or why. Assume that anonymous or un-
traceable claims are false until proven otherwise.

The Hoax

This version was forwarded to FactCheck.org in 2006, but it's been around since 2001 and is only one of many we've been asked about.

Anyone remember this??

It was 1987! At a lecture the other day they were playing an old news video of Lt. Col. Oliver North testifying at the Iran-Contra hearings during the Reagan Administration.

There was Ollie in front of God and country getting the third degree, but what he said was stunning!

He was being drilled by a senator; "Did you not recently spend close to $60,000 for a home security system?"

Ollie replied, "Yes, I did, Sir."

The senator continued, trying to get a laugh out of the audience, "Isn't that just a little excessive?"

"No, sir," continued Ollie.

"No? And why not?" the senator asked.

"Because the lives of my family and I were threatened, sir."

"Threatened? By whom?" the senator questioned.

"By a terrorist, sir" Ollie answered.

"Terrorist? What terrorist could possibly scare you that much?"

"His name is Osama bin Laden, sir" Ollie replied.

At this point the senator tried to repeat the name, but couldn't pronounce it, which most people back then probably couldn't. A couple of people laughed at the attempt. Then the senator continued. Why are you so afraid of this man?" the senator asked.

"Because, sir, he is the most evil person alive that I know of", Ollie answered.

"And what do you recommend we do about him?" asked the senator.

"Well, sir, if it was up to me, I would recommend that an assassin team be formed to eliminate him and his men from the face of the earth."

The senator disagreed with this approach, and that was all that was shown of the clip.

By the way, that senator was Al Gore!

The Disproof

These are images of the transcript of North's actual testimony, taken from the official website of the U.S. Senate, at www.senate.gov/reference/resources/pdf/ollie.pdf:

IRAN-CONTRA INVESTIGATION

JOINT HEARINGS
BEFORE THE

SENATE SELECT COMMITTEE ON SECRET
MILITARY ASSISTANCE TO IRAN AND
THE NICARAGUAN OPPOSITION

AND THE

HOUSE SELECT COMMITTEE
TO INVESTIGATE COVERT ARMS
TRANSACTIONS WITH IRAN

ONE HUNDREDTH CONGRESS

FIRST SESSION

100-7

Part I

JULY 7, 8, 9, AND 10, 1987

TESTIMONY OF OLIVER L. NORTH
(Questioning by Counsels)

Printed for the use of the Select Committees on the Iran-Contra Investigation

U.S. GOVERNMENT PRINTING OFFICE

75-544   WASHINGTON : 1988

For sale by the Superintendent of Documents, U.S. Government Printing Office
Washington, DC 20402

–EXCERPT OF COL. OLIVER NORTH'S TESTIMONY
ON SECURITY FENCE AND ABU NIDAL–

129

al Secord, and my question to you is, were you aware—I take it
there was a security system put in at your residence?
   Mr. NORTH. There is a security system in at my residence. It has
since this April been sufficiently supplemented that it is now extraordinary.
   Mr. NIELDS. And I take it——
   [Counsel conferring with witness.]
   Mr. NIELDS. Were you aware that that security system was paid
for by General Secord?
   Mr. NORTH. I am going to waffle an answer. I am going to say
yes and no, and if you would indulge me, I will give you another
one of my very straightforward, but rather lengthy, answers.
   The issue of the security system was first broached immediately
after a threat on my life by Abu Nidal. Abu Nidal is, as I am sure
you on the Intelligence Committees know, the principal, foremost
assassin in the world today. He is a brutal murderer. When I was

Look instead for sources with authority. The U.S. Senate's historian is, obviously, an excellent source with respect to the Ollie North affair. When the Senate website posts pages from the official transcript of those hearings, you can be close to 100 percent certain that what you're reading is what North really said. North's own website is another good source, because the information is coming from North himself, and also because he is about the last person we'd expect to lie to protect a Democrat.

Government websites have as much authority and credibility as the agencies that stand behind them. To get the latest official estimate of the U.S. population, you can now go directly to the website of the Census Bureau, where you will also find official measures of poverty, income, the number of persons with and without health insurance, and much more. The figures we cited for causes of death among women came directly from the website of the National Center for Health Statistics, where the federal government posts its official tally of death records from all fifty states. And our figures showing the tiny percentage of affluent Americans who actually pay estate tax came from the website of the Internal Revenue Service, which publishes data taken directly from the tens of millions of tax forms it processes each year. At the National Aeronautics and Space Administration's website, you can find authoritative information on what scientists know about the solar system and the universe, including the latest on the expected recovery of the earth's protective ozone layer.

Look for a "dot-gov" extension on the website's address. For example, www.socialsecurity.gov is the home page of the U.S. Social Security Administration, where you can find the latest statistics on the system's financial troubles, provided by its board of trustees. There you will see that, unless Washington acts, benefits will have to be cut, or taxes increased, in 2040. You can also run down the most popular names for babies. In applications for Social Security cards, parents in 2005 chose Emily for girls and Jacob for boys more often than any other names. The dot-gov extension also can be used by state governments. For example, at www.ohio.gov you can see who's governor or read the state constitution or laws, and at the Ohio State Highway Patrol's site you can even get a satellite map of all the fatal car, truck, and motorcycle crashes in the state in 2005. That last may or may not be particularly useful, but since it comes from the Ohio State Highway Patrol, you can be reasonably sure it's correct.

We would never suggest that everything you find on a dot-gov website should be believed, of course. Apply thought and common sense, as you would anywhere else.

At www.whitehouse.gov, for example, you will find the words that President Bush has spoken at his public appearances, officially transcribed and in full context. You can be reasonably confident that those are Bush's exact words; the incidents where reporters' tapes differ from the official transcript are rare. But it's still up to you to decide whether you believe what Bush said. And also be careful when using House and Senate websites. For example, www.dems.gov takes you to the website of the House Democratic Caucus, made up of all the Democrats in the House, just as www.gop.gov takes you to the House Republican Conference. These partisan websites will tell you much about the current party line, but can't be expected to give a balanced account of the facts.

Most official House and Senate committee websites have been even worse, seeming to speak for the full committee but in fact posting only talking points for the party in the majority and omitting mention of the minority party's views. In 2006, www.waysandmeans.gov was run by Republicans, who controlled the House and the tax-writing Ways and Means Committee along with it. So it should be no surprise that the committee website contained a misleading press release praising a Republican bill that "would permanently eliminate the estate tax for 99.7 percent of all Americans." That's misleading because you can't really "eliminate" a tax for the 99 percent who weren't liable for it in the first place.* That release was typical of the slanted information on taxes and Republican-sponsored tax cuts that appeared on the committee's website.

With Republicans in control, reaching the site run by the Democrats on the Ways and Means Committee required a visitor to find the link labeled "Minority Website," which appeared in tiny 8-point type hidden away near the bottom of the page. And the same went for nearly all other House and Senate committee websites: they spoke only for the majority party. When Democrats are in control these official sites may or may not become less partisan, so visitors should continue to be wary of them.

Not all committee sites were so one-sided. Two laudable exceptions were the Joint Committee on Taxation, which maintained a bipartisan staff of experts to estimate the effects of proposed tax bills on the federal budget, and the Congressional Budget Office, which did the same for a wide array of bills and government programs. That's something we hope will continue, but visitors should be alert for any changes as partisan control of Congress shifts.

Websites sponsored by academic institutions can contain a wealth of solid information. Here look for the "dot-edu" extension on the domain name, as in nahic.ucsf.edu. This is the website of the National Adolescent Health Information Center (NAHIC), which is associated with the department of pediatrics at the University of California–San Francisco. The "edu" in the domain name is short for "education," and only universities, colleges, and other accredited institutions of higher learning are allowed to use it. Research librarians searching the Internet for information on a new topic will often limit their searches to dot-edu and dot-gov websites, knowing they are much more likely to find authoritative infor-

* In 2006, it was estimated that only 0.3 percent of those who died that year would be subject to the estate tax, because the first $2 million of each estate was excluded from taxation. In 1999, only the first $600,000 was excluded, and the richest 1.3 percent paid tax, as noted in Chapter 3.

mation there than on a dot-com or dot-org website, which anybody can own.

However, the dot-edu extension is no guarantee of accuracy. Consider the example of Michael Bellesiles's book on guns, discussed previously. Professors often post their current research papers on their own pages within the website of the college or university where they teach; while such papers can be excellent resources, they are also the work of only that one professor, and don't carry the weight of the institution. Some colleges even give students personal web pages along with their dorm rooms and gym cards, and those pages all have dot-edu extensions too. If you find something on a university website that seems to contain the information you need, dig a little until you are satisfied that it was put there by experts you can trust, not by a freshman who's about to flunk out.

News organizations also run websites—for example, www.cnn.com and www.nytimes.com. In general, you can trust these sites to the same degree you would trust the news organizations that stand behind them. The BBC News website is superb for international news often ignored by U.S. news organizations. There's no need to dismiss a news story just because it appears on the website of a local or regional newspaper: the website of the New Orleans *Times-Picayune* was among the very best sources of information for what was actually happening during the Hurricane Katrina disaster in 2005, for example. For three days, the newspaper published only on the Web, because its printing plant was underwater, and eventually the quality of its reporting earned its staff two Pulitzer Prizes, including a gold medal for meritorious public service and the prize for reporting of breaking news. In this case, the information on a local newspaper's website was far superior to that found on the government websites of, for example, FEMA and the Army Corps of Engineers.

Local newspapers also carry dispatches from The Associated Press, which still sets the standard for balanced, just-the-facts reporting of current events, at least in our view. (We may be a bit biased about The AP, because Brooks Jackson worked there until 1980.) A story with an AP byline carries The AP's authority, in addition to that of the newspaper that published it. For recent events, try using Google, Yahoo, or any other good Internet search engine that can limit the search to "news." This should bring up any recent stories that contain the key words you have entered; frequently, the results will include several copies of the same AP story as reprinted in different places. However, these searches will also dredge up posts on all sorts of strongly partisan or ideological websites and blogs that can't necessarily be trusted to give a full or even an accurate account.

Free news sites have their limitations. Some require an annoying "registration" process that requires you to hand over personal information, such as your age, sex, and (in some cases) even your income. That information can be sold or otherwise used to target you for commercial purposes. You may want to check the stated "privacy policy" first, or look for the same story on another site.

A more serious weakness of Internet news searches is that most news sites charge a fee for access to stories more than about a week old. That's understandable, given the huge expense of gathering and editing those stories, but often it's impractical for the everyday user to find an older news story quickly. TV networks are especially difficult to search. They got in the habit of charging money for written transcripts of their news broadcasts long ago, and most still don't post such transcripts on their websites, except for special interviews. Notable exceptions are CNN, the BBC, and NBC News's *Meet the Press* program.

To do a thorough search of news from last month or last year, you need access to the excellent services of either Nexis or Factiva, both of which carry the full text of nearly every major newspaper, magazine, and wire service story for the past two decades. The services can be quite expensive: Nexis charges nonsubscribers $3 for every news story paid for by credit card, for example. Check your local library, which may have Nexis or Factiva access for free or at a reduced price. The online services of many college and uni-

Some FactCheck Favorites

Amid all the deception and misinformation on the Internet, some sites stand out as mostly reliable and unbiased. Here are just a few of the many we at FactCheck.org have found useful. All are free, unless otherwise noted.

www.cdc.gov

The National Center for Health Statistics, of the Centers for Disease Control, has official data on births, deaths, accidental injuries, marriages, and divorces. The "FastStats" feature allows easy location by topic.

www.ConsumerReports.org

The online version of *Consumer Reports* magazine, publishing unbiased test reports since 1936 on products of all sorts, from autos to kitchen appliances. Published by the nonprofit Consumers Union, which accepts no advertising or even free test samples. A $26 annual subscription can prevent mistakes costing much more.

www.opensecrets.org

The Center for Responsive Politics is a private, nonprofit group that collects official data on political donations and lobbying and provides useful analyses of which interest groups gave most.

www.cbo.gov

Lawmakers of both parties rely on the Congressional Budget Office for analysis of economic trends, federal spending, and the deficit, and of the likely impact of any new legislation.

www.kff.org

The Kaiser Family Foundation, whose stated mission is to "help improve health policies and programs for people in greatest need," provides a wealth of nonpartisan information about Medicare, Medicaid, private health insurance, AIDS, and women's health.

www.bls.gov

The Bureau of Labor Statistics collects official statistics on unemployment, jobs, inflation, and wages.

www.census.gov

The U.S. Census Bureau site supplies official statistics on population counts, poverty, household income, health insurance coverage, and home ownership.

www.eia.doe.gov

The Energy Information Administration has official statistics on all sources of energy, including gasoline prices, sources of crude oil, nuclear power, and solar power. The "Kids Page," more sophisticated than it sounds, provides basic summaries.

www.quackwatch.org

Dr. Stephen Barrett's respected and thoroughly documented "guide to Quackery, Health Fraud, and Intelligent Decisions" about medicine.

www.gao.gov

The Government Accountability Office is a hard-nosed, nonpartisan watchdog agency set up by Congress. The site contains reports on "high risk" programs vulnerable to fraud, waste, and mismanagement. A page on "our nation's fiscal outlook" explains why GAO believes policy changes are needed to avoid "unsustainable federal deficits and debt" in the future.

versity libraries also have subscriptions that can be used for free by faculty, students, or other authorized users.

We like to think that FactCheck.org falls into the category of trustworthy websites such as those cited in the box above. Remember, however, that even the best websites can make mistakes. In fact, one way to test whether a site is trustworthy is to note how it treats errors. Does it correct them quickly and openly? Never rely on only one source for important information; look for two or three that are independent of each other.

A word about the very popular online encyclopedia Wikipedia,

which we have not listed as
one of our trustworthy sites.
We've found it to be a conve-
nient place to start research-
ing an unfamiliar subject,
and we refer to it often ourselves. But we would never
rely on it as an authoritative source because anybody
can edit Wikipedia at any
time, and there are numer-

A Guide to Websites

A great online guide to finding reliable
websites is the Librarians' Internet Index,
www.lii.org. It links to thousands of
websites that have been screened by
professional librarians—people who look
things up for a living. Its more than
20,000 entries are organized under
14 main topics and nearly 300 related
topics.

ous documented instances of mistakes or deliberate misinformation appearing there. Any information found on Wikipedia must be
used with caution and considered subject to verification.

Even wholly biased and partisan sources can be trusted in
some respects. The website of a political candidate can tell you exactly what the candidate's current TV ads are saying, or what his or
her current position is on a particular issue. It won't, however, tell
you whether those TV ads are true or false, or whether the candidate previously took a different position and then flip-flopped. By
the same token, the website of a product's manufacturer might be
a good source for the product's list price, its technical specifica-
tions, and perhaps even reprints of independent reviews of the
product—positive reviews, that is. But don't expect to find information on safety defects, or independent reviews that recommend a
cheaper, better product made by another company.

Blogs can also be useful, but, not surprisingly, they tend to reflect the biases of their creators. In its simplest form, a blog is a personal diary posted for all to see. Anyone can start a new one in
minutes at little or no cost, using any one of several services. And
many have done so. Technorati.com says it detects 1.6 million new
blog postings *per day*. Blogging is just a pastime for most; 84 percent of bloggers surveyed by the Pew Internet & American Life
Project in 2006 called it either a "hobby" or just "something I do,

but not something I spend a lot of time on." Only about one in
three consider their blogs a form of journalism, and 42 percent say
they "never" or "hardly ever" spend extra time trying to verify statements that appear on their blogs. So never accept something as fact
just because it appears on somebody's blog; check it out for yourself.

It's true that some blogs have had a big political impact. Daily
Kos, a site founded by Markos Moulitsas, was a force behind Howard Dean's 2004 presidential campaign, and it claimed to have
raised more than $1 million for a dozen liberal congressional candi-
dates running in 2004. It's also true that a number of bloggers offer
opinion and commentary as well written as any you'll find in the
opinion pages of major newspapers and magazines. Some mainstream journalists also blog. The best bloggers read widely and
bring to their journals a collection of links to the most interesting
items they've found, making some blogs a fine place to keep up on
what's being said about certain subjects in a lot of different places.
That's especially true for politics. The Pew poll found that 11 percent of bloggers say they deal primarily with politics and government.

However, it's rare to find solid, original reporting on a blog. The
most celebrated example is still the 2004 coup scored by the conservative website Little Green Footballs, whose owner, with help
from other like-minded bloggers, quickly exposed as likely forgeries
some documents used by CBS News's Dan Rather to back up a report that President Bush had shirked his duties as a young pilot in
the Texas Air National Guard. The memos were supposedly written
by Bush's commanding officer in 1973. Within hours of the CBS
broadcast, LGF's Charles Johnson produced a seemingly exact
match for one of the memos using the standard settings on Microsoft Word and a computer printer, technology that didn't come
into widespread use until the 1990s. The memos included effects
such as proportional spacing and a superscript (the "th" in "187th"),
and even today we know of nobody who has reproduced the CBS

memos using the office technology of 1973. Nearly all experts believe the documents were fakes.

Sometimes an individual blogger can go places and see things that news reporters can't; notable for this were the Iraqi and U.S. military bloggers who posted personal journals of life in Iraq, and the bloggers who were on the scene of the earthquake and tsunami of December 26, 2004. Other blogs have evolved into mini–news organizations, employing small staffs of professional reporters and writers. We found TPM Muckraker a fine place to follow Washington corruption scandals as they unfolded during 2006, for example. The site's staff cast a wide net for bits of new information—an exclusive interview in a San Diego newspaper, a little-noticed affidavit from a government investigator filed in a Washington, D.C., courthouse—and presented them in one place along with thoughtful and careful speculation about the possible implications. Even though it was established by a liberal website, Talking Points Memo, the Muckraker site was equally vigorous in following the legal troubles of both Republicans and Democrats. It provided more detailed and up-to-the-minute coverage of the congressional scandals than we found in any other place. But unbiased, professional-quality news blogs are rare, and the unwary blog reader can still be taken in by spectacular mistakes such as truthout.org's "exclusive" report of Karl Rove's "indictment," mentioned earlier, or the rumor-has-it style of "reporting" favored by Matt Drudge (the Drudge Report) and his imitators.

It bears repeating: something stated as a fact on a blog might be true, or it might not. Verify it elsewhere. Often bloggers provide links to the source of their information, which can be helpful. But sometimes those links just lead to another blog, which may or may not have provided a link to the original source.

Due Diligence

There's more to evaluating a website than figuring out whether it is sponsored by a government agency, a university think tank or scholar, or just some crank, however. As we've shown, even a government site can turn out to contain little more than the talking points of the political party that controls it, and a lone blogger can—sometimes—have better evidence than an entire network news organization. Weighing the trustworthiness of any particular website requires a bit of what investors and lawyers call due diligence. That means checking out the management and finances before you buy. It's like checking the reputation of a prospective date, or running the statistics on a prospective player for a fantasy football team. Due diligence is usually just a matter of answering a few questions.

Take, for example, the growth hormone scams that litter the Internet. Perhaps you have received an e-mail message like one sent in 2005 that touted a dietary supplement, HGH 5000, claiming it could "Reduce Body Fat and Build Lean Muscle WITHOUT EXERCISE." Skeptical, you want to dig for the facts about this seemingly miraculous product. How would you do that? What questions would you ask? Typing "HGH" into an Internet search engine would be the first step, and that would bring up scores of websites, some of which claim to be "buyer's guides" or "consumer reviews" giving out unbiased information about this product. Some quote medical doctors praising the "clinically proven" benefits of HGH, and many cite an article in *The New England Journal of Medicine* as proof. All this sounds pretty good—until you start asking questions.

- What are they selling? Scroll down the page on any of these pro-HGH sites and you quickly find they are actually just online stores selling an expensive product. (HGH typically costs $30–$60 or so for a one-month supply.) You can order the "recommended" product directly. That should be a tip-off that the site's information is biased. After all, you wouldn't expect a political candidate's site to give you a fair account of the opponent's virtues. Websites that are selling something, whether it's a product, a candidate, or a public policy, are necessarily one-sided at best, and often downright misleading.

• What's their reputation? At the Federal Trade Commission's website, we find a "consumer alert" warning us about HGH products. It says that while there "may" be some benefits from real, prescription-only human growth hormone, "FTC staff has seen no reliable evidence to support the claim that these 'wannabe' products [advertised on the Internet] have the same effect as prescription HGH." The FTC is a federal agency with a good reputation for protecting consumers from false advertising, and so we should trust this mild warning much more than the sites that stand to profit from selling us this product. And the FTC is being bureaucratically cautious. Search a bit more and you may find the independent website Quackwatch, one of our favorites, which tells us that the thousands of physicians marketing themselves as "anti-aging specialists" are really practicing an unrecognized specialty, that shots of real HGH for normal people "appear to be a very poor investment," and that the products being sold without prescription are outright fakes. We trust Quackwatch because it has been working to expose various medical frauds since 1969 (before there were even websites) and was listed by *The Journal of the American Medical Association* in 1998 as one of nine sites providing "reliable health information and resources." With a reputation like that, we'd accept anything Quackwatch says over the word of anybody trying to sell us a modern Fountain of Youth.

• Can I verify? Look for footnotes and links to original source material. These allow you to "drill down" to find out more and to verify claims for yourself. Huckster websites tend to make claims that the reader can't check independently. They refer vaguely to "studies," without saying who published them or how they were conducted, and they provide "testimonials" by unnamed persons who can't be contacted. Politicians likewise love to cite "studies" to prove their points, but a closer look often shows that the studies don't really provide the support claimed, or that they come from a hopelessly biased source. HGH provides a perfect example of why one should verify important claims at their source. The product's hucksters cite a 1990 article in *The New England Journal of Medicine* to support their claim that real human growth hormone has been "clinically proven" to have all sorts of anti-aging properties. But they generally don't provide a link to that article, and for good reason. Find it for yourself: search the Web for "New England Journal" plus "human growth," and up will come a warning that "this article has been cited in potentially misleading" advertising. You find that the original study involved only a dozen men who actually got injections of the hormone, all over sixty years old and all with unusually low levels of the insulin-like "growth factor 1." They got injections of real, prescription-only hormone three times per week. This is no proof that younger people, or persons with normal levels of the substance, would see any benefit. The online article now includes a link to a 2003 editorial in which the *Journal* calls that study "biologically interesting" but "not sufficient to serve as a basis for treatment recommendations." In other words, a closer look shows the hucksters are simply misrepresenting the published research. President Ronald Reagan once said famously of the Soviet Union, "Trust, but verify." When it comes to the Internet, we advise an even tougher attitude: *don't* trust unless you *can* verify.

False Quotes

The Internet teems with unverified "quotes" supposedly uttered by famous people. Some of these attributions, perhaps many, are false.

For example, we heard a nice remark by Albert Einstein that we thought might fit in this book: "Information is not knowledge." We take that to mean that raw facts mean little unless we validate them, think about them logically, and follow them to a valid conclusion. Sage advice, but none of the many Internet citations we found told us when the great physicist gave it, or where, or to whom. Did he say it in a lecture, a book, a letter to a colleague, or an interview? Was it a casual remark to a friend or colleague, who mentioned it later in his or her own writings?

We checked with Barbara Wolff at the Albert Einstein Archives of the Jewish National and University Library in Jerusalem, where the physicist's surviving personal papers and writings are housed. She told us: "The quote in question is not known to me, and was not found among Einstein's identifiable quotes."

How could so many people make the mistake of falsely attributing the words to Einstein? Ms. Wolff has a theory, with which we agree: "As, unfortunately, it happens again and again, someone might have composed a more or less meaningful aphorism, and, anticipating that his own name would not draw attention to it, simply foisted it on Einstein." Be careful about any quotation whose source can't be verified. Sometimes the person quoted never really said it.

- Who's behind it? If you're unfamiliar with the organization sponsoring a website, start with the "About Us" link and learn what the group says about its mission, political leanings, and finances. An anonymous website should be treated just like an anonymous e-mail: don't believe a word you find there unless it's verified independently. If you are looking for information about whether raising the federal minimum wage benefits workers or costs jobs, you quickly find that torrents of information pour out of two organizations with the same initials and very similar names, the Economic Policy Institute and the Employment Policies Institute. One EPI is pro-labor; it cites statistics about how inflation chips away at the buying power of a minimum-wage paycheck and how many families would benefit from an increase. The other EPI is pro-business; it posts studies estimating the number of low-wage workers who will be laid off, or not hired in the first place, if businesses are forced to pay more. The Economic Policy Institute says of itself that it "stresses . . . a concern for the living standards of working people," and it lists as its chairman Gerald W. McEntee, president of the American Federation of State, County and Municipal Employees. The other EPI is less forthcoming, calling itself "a non-profit research organization dedicated to studying public policy issues surrounding employment growth." The word "growth" is a tip-off, however. It's a favorite buzzword among free-market groups. And the group's executive director is Richard Berman, who (we can discover by plugging his name into our search engine) is a Washington public relations man who was once an executive vice president of the Pillsbury Restaurant Group, owner of the Burger King chain, which employs thousands of low-wage workers. The fact that one of the EPIs is labor-backed and the other is business-backed doesn't make either of them right or wrong, but it does mean that neither is a neutral source. Knowing which is which helps us evaluate their one-sided information and arguments. In general, the less a website tells you about itself in its "About Us" section, the less you should trust it.

• Who's paying? Where an organization gets its money can tell you a lot about its leanings. The Progress and Freedom Foundation, for example, describes itself straightforwardly as a "market-oriented think tank" studying the "digital revolution," and it openly lists the many corporations that support it financially, including Apple, Microsoft, Comcast, and other computer, cable TV, and Internet companies. The Clean and Safe Energy Coalition was launched in April 2006 by a co-founder of Greenpeace; it argues that more nuclear reactors would be good for the environment because they don't put out smoke or greenhouse gasses. In the fine print, you'll find that the "coalition" is funded by the Nuclear Energy Institute, a trade group for the industry. Industry funding doesn't mean a group's information is wrong, but it is likely to reflect the business side.

• Who are the people? Sometimes the people at an organization are a clue to what's up. The Center for American Progress describes itself as "a nonpartisan research and educational institute," for example, but the people behind it amount to a Democratic administration in exile. CAP's president and CEO is John Podesta, who was Bill Clinton's last White House chief of staff, and top positions are filled almost exclusively by Democrats, including former aides to Clinton, Senator Ted Kennedy, and former House Democratic leader Dick Gephardt. That doesn't look very "nonpartisan" to us. Contrast that group to the Institute for International Economics, a leading think tank on the global economy. It professes to be "nonpartisan" and really is. Its board of directors includes many big names from both major parties: its chairman is Peter G. Peterson, a Republican who was once secretary of commerce under Richard Nixon, and another member is former senator Bill Bradley, who ran for the Democratic presidential nomination in 2000. The same goes for Resources for the Future, an environmental think tank headed by former Democratic congressman Phil Sharp of Indiana, but which also has a

genuinely bipartisan board including such well-known
Republicans as R. Glenn Hubbard, former head of
George W. Bush's Council of Economic Advisers, and
former representative Jim Greenwood of Pennsylvania.

There are other tests you can use to evaluate a website. Is the
information current? Check when the page you are reading was last
updated. Some sites haven't been kept up for years, yet remain on
the Internet like a virtual ghost town. Do obvious misspellings,
grammatical mistakes, or other errors demonstrate a general care-
lessness? Is the writing clear and easy to understand? Does the author have sufficient education or background? If the author is
stating opinions, are they clearly labeled as such? Does the website
correct its own errors openly? Is the author plagiarizing? (You can
check for that by plugging any unusual phrases into your search engine to see where else they might pop up.)

Finding the good stuff on the Web is a skill that grows with experience. As a start, try looking for information about Dr. Martin
Luther King, Jr. One of the sites an Internet search for his name
brings up as we write this is actually sponsored by a white suprema-
cist organization. See if you can tell which one, and which former
leader of the Ku Klux Klan is behind it. (If you have trouble, you
might want to check out a fine little animated tutorial on evaluating
websites. Prepared by the library staff at Widener University, it
uses the racist King site as an example. Go to www.widener.edu
and click "Libraries" at the bottom of the page to reach the Wolf-
gram Memorial Library home page, then click "Evaluate Web
Pages" to reach the tutorial.)

Your search for King can also bring up transcripts of King's actual papers, sermons, and speeches, compiled by the Stanford University historian Clayborne Carson, director of the King Papers
Project, and presented on the university's website. This is the next
best thing to holding King's original letters in your hand or listening
to unedited recordings of his speeches. That's the Internet for

you—learn to sidestep the booby traps, and you'll find enormous stores of high-quality information.

Then what? How certain can you be of any given fact, however authoritative the source may be? How do you tell the important facts from the not so important? How do you draw valid conclusions from the information you have? Those subjects we turn to in our next chapter.

Chapter 8

Was Clarence Darrow
a Creationist?

How to Be Sure

SOMETIMES EVEN THE MOST AUTHORITATIVE SOURCE CAN LET US
down, making it risky to rely on any single informant. To be certain
of our facts—or as certain as we can be in an uncertain world—we
often need to question, track back, and cross-check. To avoid error
requires a bit of simple mental discipline, but adopting the proper
thinking habits doesn't take a genius IQ or even a lot of work, and
can save us from looking foolish.

We offer the example of the creationists who thought they had
found an ally in the legendary attorney Clarence Darrow, because
of a remark attributed to him by an article in the *Yale Law Journal*.
The Darrow "quote" was repeated countless times, year after year, in
books, articles, speeches, sermons, and even newspaper stories. But
there's no evidence Darrow ever said it.

Darrow was the lawyer who in 1925 had defended John
Scopes against the charge that he had broken Tennessee law by

teaching Darwinism. Supposedly, Darrow said it was "bigotry for public schools to teach only one theory of origins." Creationists argued that banning the teaching of their religiously based ideas in public schools was "Scopes in reverse," motivated by anti-Christian bias. Now here was the evolutionists' own hero saying, in effect, that those who wanted only evolution taught in public schools were "bigots."

The person who tracked the trumped-up quotation back to its dubious source was a UCLA graduate student named Tom McIver, who published an exhaustively researched, 5,000-word article in *Creation/Evolution,* a publication of the American Humanist Association. He starts his account with the 1982 book *The Creator in the Courtroom: "Scopes II,"* whose creationist author, Norman Geisler, attributed the remark only to "Clarence Darrow: Scopes Trial, 1925." From there, McIver traced the quote back to a 1978 article in the *Yale Law Journal* by a creationist lawyer, Wendell Bird, whom many other creationists cited as their source. The *Yale Law Journal* article in turn cited an article from a 1974 symposium at Bryan College, a Bible-based institution in Dayton, Tennessee, the city where the Scopes trial was held. The author of that article was Robert O'Bannon, a biology professor at Lee College (now Lee University) in Cleveland, Tennessee. He in turn cited a 1974 article in a now defunct magazine called *Science and Scripture.* The author of *that* article was Jolly F. Griggs, a California creationist.

But what was Griggs's source? Nowhere in the actual transcript of the Scopes trial does such a remark appear. Griggs admitted to McIver that he had no documentation and said he hadn't even meant to treat the words as a direct quote. He said he had meant to paraphrase something he remembered being told years earlier by a Baptist preacher in Denver. Griggs thought the preacher might have seen the quote in a Dayton newspaper around the time of the trial, but the preacher had since died. And there the trail ended: with the quotation exposed as a half-remembered story told by a dead man who might or might not have seen it in a newspaper around 1925, and might or might not have recalled it correctly decades later.

We think the chances that Darrow ever said anything like it are vanishingly small. The transcript of the Scopes trial shows that Darrow used the words "bigotry" and "bigot" a lot, but not in a way creationists would find comforting. For example, when the opposing counsel, William Jennings Bryan, accused him of being out "to cast ridicule on everybody who believes in the Bible," Darrow shot back: "We have the purpose of preventing bigots and ignoramuses from controlling the education of the United States and you know it, and that is all."

Responsible creationists no longer use the bogus Darrow quotation. Norman Geisler wrote, "I wish to commend Tom McIver for exposing the questionable authenticity" of the words he had once attributed to Darrow. Geisler also said that Bird, the author of the *Yale Law Journal* article, recognized now that the quote is "probably not authentic." And yet plenty of creationists and "intelligent design" advocates still use this spurious quotation, nearly two decades after McIver's 1988 article exposed it as a fantasy.

How Can We Know?

How could an undocumented quote be so widely accepted as accurate? McIver thinks those who swallowed the quote fell into a psychological trap like those we spoke of in Chapter 4: "It says what they want to believe, so they assume it is true." But we think there's a larger question here. How can we ever be certain of our facts when even the *Yale Law Journal* can turn out to be wrong? What should we do to avoid being misled? Clearly, finding facts in a world of disinformation requires something more than just relying on generally reliable websites, or generally reliable books, newspapers, or encyclopedias, or factual sources of any description, for that matter. We'll spend the rest of this chapter giving you some of the general rules we follow at FactCheck.org.

RULE #1: *You Can't Be* Completely *Certain*

THE FIRST THING TO REALIZE IS THAT ABSOLUTE CERTAINTY IS ELU-sive, especially in the practical domains with which we have been dealing in this book. We are not speaking of pure logic or mathematics, where 1 1 1 always equals 2. Nor are we dealing with faith-based beliefs, which generally aren't subject to scientific proof or disproof. In fact, we should be suspicious of any claims that something is "always" or "never" so. How can you be certain?

You might think that all swans are white because you have never seen a black one. But there are black swans, in Australia. Karl Popper, a famous philosopher who died in 1994, held that even the so-called laws of science are hypothetical, subject to being disproved someday by new evidence. You only need one counterexample to disprove a claim of "never" or "always." All swans are white—until you see a black one. But you never can tell when that might happen.

Everybody craves certainty, if only because living with doubt is psychologically uncomfortable and gets in the way of deciding what to do. That's why we often fall into the "I know I'm right" trap we mentioned in Chapter 4. CIA director George Tenet did that when he

---

"Slam Dunk," Then and Now

THEN:

PRESIDENT BUSH (*Dec. 21, 2002*): "I've been told all this intelligence about having WMD, and this is the best we've got?"

CIA DIRECTOR GEORGE TENET: "It's a slam-dunk case."

BUSH: "George, how confident are you?"

TENET: "Don't worry, it's a slam dunk."

—quoted by Bob Woodward in his book *Plan of Attack*

NOW:

TENET: "Those were the two dumbest words I ever said."

—quoted by The Associated Press, in a speech at Kutztown University on April 28, 2005

expressed absolute confidence that Iraq had weapons of mass destruction. But experience shows it's wise to practice "active openmindedness." Tenet certainly wishes *he* had.

Perfect knowledge is seldom if ever available to humans. For one thing, new information is constantly arriving, and human learning is constantly expanding. How certain are we of that? Quite certain—which leads us to:

RULE #2: *You* Can *Be Certain* Enough

IN THE WORLD OF PRACTICAL REALITY, WEIGHING THE FACTS IS A matter of choosing the right standard of proof to give us the degree of certainty we need under the circumstances. We can't be absolutely certain, but we can be certain enough to make a reasonable decision. A civil jury in Santa Monica was certain enough in 1997, for example, that O. J. Simpson will never find "the real killer" of his wife, Nicole Simpson, and her friend Ronald Goldman because *he's* the real killer. But sixteen months earlier, a criminal jury in Los Angeles found him not guilty of the same crimes in one of the most celebrated trials of the twentieth century. Both votes were unanimous.

How can that be? A big reason is that our laws require proof of guilt "beyond a reasonable doubt" in a criminal case. That is—quite appropriately—a very high standard, and it applies because that's how "certain enough" we need to be before depriving anyone of his or her liberty or very life. But in a civil trial, a lower standard applies because only property is at stake. The twelve-person jury in the civil trial unanimously found that a "preponderance" of the evidence showed Simpson killed Goldman and committed battery upon Nicole, whose throat was slashed.

In our everyday lives, we have to pick an appropriate standard. Imagine trying to prove "beyond a reasonable doubt" whether one brand of cornflakes is better than another. You would never get breakfast! But the more important the decision, and the more difficult it is to reverse the consequences of that decision, the more careful we have to be.

Carpenters and seamstresses have a saying: "Measure twice, cut once." It's one thing to guess or use trial and error with respect to trivial matters or decisions that can easily be reversed, but you should try for a higher degree of certainty before buying a car or a house, and a higher degree still when choosing a spouse or a president. The research on this point is reassuring: when confronted with decisions that are significant and irreversible, people do tend to be more analytical, and to take more time thinking about the decision. Be as certain as you need to be.

Johnson's Rock

A note to our academic friends: We don't hold with the philosophical notion that maintains there are no facts, only subjective interpretations. That's a fine subject for debate in the classroom or an all-night bull session in the dorm, but it isn't much use in the everyday world.

We stand with the eighteenth-century English writer Samuel Johnson. His biographer James Boswell said he told Johnson it wasn't possible to refute Bishop Berkeley's "ingenious sophistry" that matter didn't exist. Boswell recalled:

"I never shall forget the alacrity with which Johnson answered, striking his foot with mighty force against a large stone, till he rebounded from it,—'I refute it *thus*.'"

That's our position. If you can kick a rock, you have verified the rock's existence as a practical fact. You have proof enough. We can't prove the sun will rise in the east tomorrow, because nobody can foretell the future. We do have evidence that it's come up in the east every day for perhaps 4 billion years, so we operate on the theory that it will rise there again tomorrow. We're certain enough we're right, and we haven't been proved wrong yet.

> ## RULE #3: *Look for General Agreement Among Experts*

SOME STATISTICS ARE SETTLED AND ACCEPTED BY ALL SIDES: Demo-crats, Republicans, and even vegetarian anarchists. The circumfer-ence of the earth is 24,901.55 miles at the equator, according to the National Aeronautics and Space Administration. We won't quibble with that. The national average price for a gallon of unleaded regu-lar gasoline was just over $3 the week ending July 24, 2006, accord-ing to the U.S. Energy Information Administration, and we know of nobody who seriously quarrels with EIA's figures. By the same token, there's hardly any disagreement with the tabulations of the Bureau of Labor Statistics that say the U.S. economy added 6.6 mil-lion payroll jobs in the three years following the depths of a job slump in August 2003, or that the unemployment rate fell from above 6 percent to as low as 4.6 percent during the same period. Economists and political pundits can debate the meaning or the significance of those BLS figures endlessly, and sometimes they de-bate the definitions and methods on which they are based. But the numbers come from two huge monthly surveys that economists generally accept as the best available measures of employment and unemployment.

Keep in mind that consensus isn't proof. Galileo demonstrated that in the seventeenth century, when he challenged nearly 2,000 years of Aristotelian thinking about physics and was proved correct. Sometimes the lone dissenter is on to something, and we should al-ways be alert to that possibility. Nevertheless, we can be much more confident that we are getting the facts right when we start with what's widely accepted by authorities on all sides.

RULE #4: *Check Primary Sources*

ANYONE WHO HAS PLAYED THE CHILDHOOD GAME OF TELEPHONE knows how messages can be garbled in retelling, just as the Darrow "quote" was transformed from an old preacher's story to a footnoted quotation in a prestigious law journal. The British tell the story of a military message sent to headquarters: "Send reinforcements, we are going to advance." After passing from one soldier to another, it supposedly arrived as "Send three and fourpence, we are going to a dance." That's no doubt fictional, but miscommunication does happen. It's always best to check secondhand accounts against the original.

Our courts recognize this principle by generally refusing to accept secondhand accounts, or "hearsay," as evidence. If Jim says he heard Joe tell about a robbery he saw somebody else commit, Jim's account isn't really good evidence. Jim could have heard it wrong, or remembered the story incorrectly, or Joe could have been joking or making it up or just mistaken. For a better idea of what happened, we need to hear Joe tell the story himself, under oath so he has a strong incentive not to lie, and we want to hear him answer questions from both sides to draw out relevant details that might help us weigh what he's saying, such as how far away he was, whether the light was good or bad, and how good his eyesight is. Even worse than hearsay are news stories based on anonymous sources, who often don't have firsthand knowledge themselves and are giving the reporter *secondhand* hearsay. And we the readers have no way of knowing who's talking, let alone how good their eyesight or hearing is, or whether they might have a motive to shade their story or just lie.

Sometimes checking primary sources is as simple as comparing a newspaper headline with what the news story actually says. Consider a Reuters story of November 16, 2005, that was headlined "Cheney says war critics 'dishonest, reprehensible.' " Similar headlines appeared in many newspapers, prompting a furious outcry against Vice President Richard Cheney. How dare he call it "dishonest" and "reprehensible" to question the wisdom of a war that was, to put it mildly, not going well? But what Cheney actually said was this: "The suggestion that's been made by some U.S. Senators that the President of the United States or any member of this administration purposely misled the American people on prewar intelligence is one of the most dishonest and reprehensible charges ever aired in this city." Cheney was referring to senators who had suggested he and the president were liars, not to "war critics" in general. There's a big difference.

Nevertheless, many lashed out at Cheney as though he had accused all who criticize the Iraq War of being dishonest scum, as implied by the Reuters headline. Later Cheney said, "I have a quarrel with that headline. . . . I do not believe it is wrong to criticize the war on terror or any aspect thereof. Disagreement, argument, and debate are the essence of democracy, and none of us should want it any other way."

As that incident shows, it's wise to get in the habit of reading news with the question in mind, "Does this story really back up the headline?" By the same token, ask whether the lead paragraph— which is nearly always written to be as dramatic as facts will allow, and sometimes a bit more—is really backed up by the details of the story. When you see a partial quote such as "dishonest" and "reprehensible," look for the full quote to see whether you think the reporter or headline writer understood the context fully.

Even a full transcript can be wrong. In January 1995, *The New York Times* reported that President Bill Clinton said in his State of the Union address that government should be "leaner and meaner." What Clinton actually said was "leaner, not meaner." Also, after Hurricane Katrina in 2005, we at FactCheck.org and other news organizations quoted David Lokey of the Federal Emergency Management Agency as denying that "New Orleans is filling up like a bowl" at the very moment when floodwaters were rising. In reality, the clueless statement had been made by Republican Senator David Vitter of Louisiana, who was standing next to Lokey at the same news conference. A CNN typist had gotten the words right but put them in the mouth of the wrong speaker. Videotape of the event showed Vitter speaking the words as he stepped in front of Lokey.

We're not saying that you should track every single fact back to its origin. That's clearly not possible. You don't have to go to the National Archives in Washington to read the original copy of the U.S. Constitution; you can read the text any number of places, including the National Archives website. You don't have to subscribe to *The New England Journal of Medicine* to get the gist of the latest medical research if you can read an accurate summary in a good newspaper, which is usually easier for nonmedical readers to understand anyway. We *are* saying that primary sources are more reliable than secondary sources. And when the inferences you will draw from the information are very important to you, it is best to check the primary source. Track your information upstream. Be wary of secondhand accounts, and even more wary of thirdhand stories.

RULE #5: *Know What Counts*

WHEN YOU SEE NUMBERS BEING USED, BE SURE YOU KNOW WHAT'S being counted, and what's not. Definitions matter. We wrote earlier about numerical flimflams—"cuts" that are really slower increases, and "average" tax breaks that are much bigger than most people will ever see. Often this sort of confusion and deception can be avoided with a clear understanding of exactly what the numbers are supposed to represent.

Even the simple act of counting becomes complicated in real life, because we have to make choices about what to count. George W. Bush is counted as our forty-third president, even though he's only the forty-second person to hold the office. Grover Cleveland is counted twice—as the twenty-second president and also as the twenty-fourth—because he served one term, was defeated, then was elected four years later to a second term. And if just counting to forty-three can be a problem, imagine what can happen when numbers get into the billions and the opportunities for massaging the count multiply accordingly.

For example, in his 2006 State of the Union address, President Bush said, "Every year of my presidency, we've reduced the growth of nonsecurity discretionary spending." But he sure hadn't reduced the growth of federal spending, which had shot up 42 percent since he first took office. Look carefully at what he was counting. The word "discretionary" excludes so-called entitlement programs, including Medicare, which is experiencing the largest expansion in its history because of Bush's addition of a prescription drug benefit. Notice also the term "nonsecurity," which excludes the entire Pentagon budget and also huge extra outlays for the wars in Iraq and Afghanistan and everything the Bush bean counters choose to sweep under the heading of "homeland security." Bush was counting only some relatively small categories of spending that hadn't risen so quickly.

Democrats play the same counting games. The Democratic National Committee ran a TV ad in advance of the speech we just mentioned, faulting Bush for "2.8 Million Manufacturing Jobs Lost," among other things. Notice the word "manufacturing." In fact, the U.S. economy had gained a net total of more than 2 million jobs since Bush's first day in office (first losing 3 million, then gaining 5 million). Most people probably aren't aware that manufacturing these days accounts for only a little more than one job out of every ten in the United States. And manufacturing had been almost the only major sector to decline under Bush's entire tenure. The DNC wasn't counting jobs in fast-growing sectors such as construction, health care, and finance.

Numerical flimflams are probably as old as numbers themselves, and we've already discussed a several of them. Still worth reading is the classic *How to Lie with Statistics,* a little book that Darrell Huff wrote more than half a century ago. Some of his examples sound quaint today. For example, he questions a claim that Yale graduates of the class of 1924 were earning an average of $25,111 a year, because that seemed far too grand a sum. Huff wrote that in 1954; the equivalent in 2006 dollars would be somewhere close to $180,000. Nevertheless, the numerical and statistical tricks Huff exposes are ageless and still in everyday use, and his style is so readable that we've tried to match it in this book.

RULE #6: *Know Who's Talking*

IF YOUR DOCTOR RECOMMENDS IT, PROTECTING YOURSELF AGAINST a heart attack or stroke by taking aspirin can cost as little as a penny a day. The aspirin reduces the likelihood that blood clots will form. However, studies have been appearing in medical journals suggesting that large numbers of patients need to be tested for "aspirin resistance" in case aspirin no longer protects them. These same studies suggest that many patients may need an aspirin substitute costing $4 a day. But who's paying for these studies? As *The Wall Street Journal* pointed out in a front-page story in April 2006, many of those raising the "aspirin resistance" alarm have financial ties to the companies that stand to profit from selling the tests and drugs. The newspaper reported that one study, which declared that "resistance" affects perhaps 30 percent of those taking aspirin, was funded by the test's maker, Accumetrics, Inc., and by Schering-Plough Corp., which sells a drug being tested for its potential benefit to patients resistant to aspirin. This funding wasn't disclosed by the medical journal that published the article.

Such financial ties should make us skeptical of the research findings. This is a clear conflict of interest. The author's private interest conflicts with his responsibility to provide unbiased, trust-worthy research—the public interest. Did the study's author, deliberately or otherwise, skew the research toward a finding that would create a profit for the sponsors, and make them more inclined to pay him to conduct future research? What other research did these companies fund, and did it come up with contrary findings that the companies suppressed? We're not saying that drug companies shouldn't finance research, or that paying for a study automatically produces the result they want. But knowing who's behind a statement is important in considering how much weight to give it.

It's not always obvious who's behind a study or a group. Until it disbanded in 2002, the "Global Climate Coalition" had a name that sounded neutral and a website showing happy children and green fields; but it was a lobby group made up of trade associations for industries including oil, chemicals, logging, agribusiness, and utilities, all of them financially motivated to avoid taxes or defeat regulation of their emissions of greenhouse gases. The groups named "Americans for Good Government," "Americans United in Support of Democracy," and "Maryland Association for Concerned Citizens" funnel donations to candidates who support Israel, according to the Center for Responsive Politics. The Alliance for Justice and the Committee for Justice sound alike, but they work for exactly opposite ends. The Alliance is a liberal group that opposed some of President George W. Bush's judicial nominees, while the Committee is a conservative group that ran TV ads supporting his Supreme Court picks. The latter was founded by C. Boyden Gray, who was White House counsel (and tennis partner) to Bush's father. Groups whose names seem to indicate support of a noble policy position ("good government" or "justice") may be committed to a specific party or industry. Beware.

Self-interest doesn't make a statement false. What an electric utility says about what's coming out of its smokestacks can be accurate, even if the company quite naturally would like to avoid paying for expensive scrubbers. And an environmental group's statements might not exaggerate the dangers and extent of pollution, even if the group does get more money by telling donors the skies are being poisoned than it would if it said the air is getting cleaner, as happens to be the case. (As we mentioned earlier, the EPA's tracking of the six major air pollutants shows a 12 percent decline in the five years ending in 2005, which amounts to a decrease of more than 19 million tons per year of volatile organic compounds, sulfur dioxide, carbon monoxide, nitrogen oxides, soot, and lead.) Both sides in the environmental debate have a clear motive to tilt the facts in one direction or the other, and so we shouldn't accept either at face value. Which brings us to:

RULE #7: *Seeing Shouldn't Necessarily Be Believing*

WHEN WE GAVE AS OUR FIRST RULE THAT YOU CAN'T BE 100 PERCENT certain of anything, you might have said to yourself, "I'm certain of what I see with my own eyes." Don't be. Researchers have found, for example, that people can rather easily be talked into seeing things that aren't there (or saying they do). In one of the most famous experiments in the history of social science, the late Solomon Asch showed lines of different lengths to groups of students and asked each to say which was longer or shorter. But only one student in each group was a test subject; the others were Asch's confederates, whom he had instructed. When the test subjects heard a majority of others say that the longer line was the shorter, they often said the same even though the opposite was obviously true. In fact, 37 percent of the subjects expressed the bogus view of the majority. In an even earlier experiment, from 1935, the social psychology pioneer Muzafer Sherif showed people in a dark room a light that was not moving. They reported that the light was moving—and, more important, they gave reports of the amount of movement that were consistent with what they had heard others report.

Personal experience can mislead us. Eyewitness testimony is notoriously unreliable even when given in court, under oath. Years of research show that witnesses regularly pick innocent "foils" from police line-ups. As we write this, 189 persons have been exonerated after DNA tests showed they had been wrongly convicted, according to the Innocence Project. And more than 70 percent of those were convicted on the basis of mistaken eyewitness testimony!

Scholars also tell us that people tend to overestimate how well they remember their own experiences. If you have siblings, you can test this by picking some major event in your family's past that you and they shared: each of you write an account, then see how well they agree. Scholars have found that an apparently distinct memory of something that occurred long ago may be a reconstruction, often a self-serving one. As distance from the event increases, memory decays.

Even very smart people misremember things. Alan Greenspan, the former chairman of the Federal Reserve Board, is by most accounts a very smart man, yet even he was surprised to find how much his own memory had shifted with respect to a crucial conference call on April 12, 1991. Greenspan had proposed lowering interest rates, but other members of the Federal Open Market Committee strongly objected and blocked the move. Bob Woodward reports in his 1994 book *The Agenda* that when Greenspan looked at a verbatim transcript of the meeting, he discovered "that his own memory was faulty and imbued with recollections that were self-interested but not true."

That somebody feels quite certain is no guarantee that his or her memory is accurate. Scholars who study the relationship between confidence and accuracy come up with mixed results. Sometimes witnesses who say they are positive are right, and sometimes they are not, and so far psychologists have only a dim understanding of why.

RULE #8: *Cross-check Everything That Matters*

BY NOW IT SHOULD BE OBVIOUS THAT RELYING ON A SINGLE SOURCE of information is a good way to be steered wrong. However, we can be more confident about a conclusion when different sources using different methods end up agreeing on it.

Different newspapers sometimes convey quite different impressions of the same event. When Governor Arnold Schwarzenegger of California appeared at a breakfast honoring Martin Luther King, Jr., in 2006, the *Oakland Tribune* reported that he got a "chilly reception" and the *San Jose Mercury News* described it as "hostile," but the *San Francisco Chronicle*'s headline cited a "surprisingly warm welcome." So which was right? The *Mercury News* story reported as follows: "After a few scattered boos, the audience listened politely to his speech and laughed at his Terminator jokes." Some of the labor union people who attended had talked of walking out to embarrass the Republican governor, but didn't. Whether that was "hostile" and "chilly" or "surprisingly warm" depends on whether you focused on the boos or the laughs. As for the word "surprisingly," "surprise" depends on who is surprised and what they were expecting. In this case, reading two or three newspapers produced a much more balanced picture of the event than reading any one headline or report.

Weighing Evidence

The rules that apply to evidence in trials give us a good starting point for thinking about how we should weigh facts in our everyday lives. We've already mentioned the weakness of hearsay and second-hand accounts and considered why we should give them much less weight than firsthand accounts or physical evidence. And we've mentioned our preference for primary sources; we like to check the

The Man in the Hole

How did the United States know it had the right man when soldiers pulled a disheveled wretch from a six-foot-deep "spider hole" in Ad-Dwar, Iraq, on December 13, 2003? How did they prove to Iraqi skeptics that Saddam Hussein had really been captured? By cross-checking and using multiple methods of verification.

The man announced, "I am Saddam Hussein, president of Iraq, and I am willing to negotiate," but maybe he was one of Saddam's doubles. First, U.S. officials had to convince themselves. Former ambassador L. Paul Bremer recalls that, after a shave and haircut, the captive looked like the right man: "There could be no doubt: the face in this photo was Saddam Hussein," Bremer writes in his book *My Year in Iraq.* Then four captured officials who had worked closely with Saddam Hussein were brought in. "Each prisoner had verified that the wizened man slouched on an army cot in that windowless room was in fact Saddam Hussein." But maybe they were protecting the real Saddam Hussein. So U.S. officials used digital voice analysis to confirm that their prisoner's voice was the same as the voice in archived recordings of the Iraqi leader, and they compared saliva swabs from the prisoner with DNA from "Saddam family samples."

To convince skeptical Iraqis, Bremer brought in a delegation from the U.S.-appointed Governing Council. "They could then confirm publicly they had seen the prisoner." That did it: delegation members betrayed no hint of doubt that it was the former tyrant who was now in U.S. custody; they even berated him for his actions as Iraq's president. "Why did you have Sayyid Muhammad al-Sadr murdered in 1999?" asked one. "Saddam Hussein, you are cursed by God," said another. "What do you say now about the mass graves?" challenged a third. The prisoner didn't bother denying his identity; instead, he justified his acts by calling his victims "criminals . . . thieves, traitors . . . Iranians." Arab news media carried compelling narratives of the meeting.

The process provides a classic instance of what scholars call "converging on certainty," when different methods all arrive at the same conclusion.

full transcript of an interview rather than rely on a paraphrase or partial quote. Here are some of the other factors we consider at FactCheck.org.

SWORN TESTIMONY People don't generally go to jail for lying to a reporter, but they can be imprisoned for perjury if they are shown to have lied under oath. For that reason, we can give greater weight to sworn testimony than to unsworn statements such as news releases, news conferences, or TV interviews. Lying to a congressional investigating committee or an FBI agent or a bank examiner can also be a criminal offense, so unsworn statements made to official inquiries also deserve weight, though not quite as much as statements made under oath.

SELF-INTEREST If somebody stands to profit (or to avoid loss), we naturally give his or her statements less weight than those of a neutral observer. We don't dismiss a statement just because it's made by a big corporation, or by a trial lawyer who stands to gain a multimillion-dollar fee by suing that corporation, but we don't accept such a statement at face value, either. We just assume that each party is probably giving us only one side of the story, and we look for additional evidence. We have to be alert to the possibility that a partisan is twisting the facts, either deliberately or because he or she is honestly blind to facts on the other side.

CONFESSIONS A statement does deserve special weight, however, when the person speaking makes a confession, or states facts contrary to his or her own interest. An example occurred when President Bush answered a question on December 12, 2005, by saying, "How many Iraqi citizens have died in this war? I would say thirty thousand, more or less, have died as a result of the initial incursion and the ongoing violence against Iraqis." His administration had previously refused to estimate civilian casualties, but now the president was in effect endorsing figures of the Iraq Body Count project, which compiles them from public, online media reports and eyewitness accounts. Bush's statement is evidence that the U.S. government can't refute the Iraq Body Count tabulation (which had risen to a minimum of more than 52,800 by January 2007). There are some higher estimates, disputed figures from the British medical journal *The Lancet,* which we'll have more to say about later. Our point here is that Bush's embrace of the Iraq Body Count figure is what lawyers call an "admission against interest"—a truth that it hurt him to say. We should count that as evidence that at least that many Iraqis had died.

REPUTATION OF THE AUTHORITY | When a medical study appears in *The New England Journal of Medicine,* we know it has gone through a systematic screening process called peer review, in which other knowledgeable scientists are asked to comment or point out possible flaws. The original author may then respond with clarifications or additional data. By contrast, we should always be skeptical of "scientific breakthroughs" that are announced at a news conference without any independent review by other experts. For example, when a news conference in 2002 proclaimed the birth of the first cloned human being (supposedly named "Eve"), it created a brief sensation. But good reporters were quick to point out that the man behind the announcement, a French former journalist named Claude Vorilhon, had renamed himself Rael, claimed to be a direct descendant of extraterrestrials who created human life on earth, and founded a cult. Neither "Eve" nor the mother of the supposedly cloned baby ever appeared publicly. Reasonable people gave the unsupported announcement zero weight and quickly dismissed it as a silly fraud.

TRANSPARENCY | Look for transparency whenever a claim is made. Is the publisher of a poll telling you the statistical margin of error and exactly how the poll takers asked the question? If not, don't give much weight to the result. Political candidates who are challenging entrenched incumbents like to release polls showing that they are "closing the gap" or even have a lead, in order to convince potential donors they can win. But such polls can be tailored to produce a positive result by including loaded questions. The challenger might ask, "Did you know the incumbent is a wife-beater?" These so-called push questions nudge the respondent toward the desired answer, and a poll containing them is called a push poll. Questions can also be worded in ways that bias the result. One survey conducted by the Annenberg Public Policy Center found a dramatic difference in support for school vouchers depending on whether such phrases as "taxpayers' money" or "private schools" were included in the question. And polls asking about support for public financing of political campaigns come out one way if the poll taker asks about "banning special-interest contributions from elections" and another if they ask about "giving tax money to politicians" as a substitute.

When reading a news story or article, ask whether the reporter or author is telling you where the information came from. We supply footnotes at FactCheck.org, with links to the sources we are using if they are available free on the Internet, so that readers may find more information or check that we're getting it right. When you see somebody claim that "a study" has backed up their claims, ask how it was conducted, how many people participated and under what conditions, and whether it really supports what's being said.

PRECISION | Sometimes evidence isn't nearly as precise as portrayed. A good example is a pair of studies that produced shocking headlines about deaths in Iraq, studies that have since been widely questioned and disparaged. Both studies were published in the British medical journal *The Lancet,* and both were produced by a team from Johns Hopkins University in Baltimore. The first was released five days before the 2004 presidential election, and estimated that 98,000 Iraqis had died as a result of the invasion ordered by President George W. Bush in March 2003. The second was released less than a month before the 2006 midterm House and Senate elections, and estimated that the Iraqi death toll had reached 654,965 from the invasion and the violent aftermath. Both were several times higher than other generally accepted estimates.

However, neither estimate was an exact count, just the midpoint of an exceptionally broad range of possibilities. For the first estimate, the authors calculated that their "confidence interval" was somewhere between 8,000 deaths and 194,000 deaths. In the language of statistics, that means a 95 percent probability that the actual figure fell somewhere within that huge range. Put another way, there was 1 chance in 40 that the actual number was less than 8,000 and an equal chance that it was greater than 194,000. As the critic Fred Kaplan put it in an article for the online magazine *Slate,* "This isn't an estimate. It's a dart board." For the second estimate the dart board was larger, between 393,000 and 943,000 deaths. Such wide ranges of uncertainty are much larger than the plus or minus 2 or 3 percent we are used to seeing in U.S. public opinion polls, and should tell us to beware.

The exceptionally imprecise estimates of the *Lancet* studies stem from the relatively small sample used to produce them. The estimates came from interviews in 33 clusters for the first study, 47 for the second. Using such randomly chosen "clusters" is a statistical method commonly used when it isn't practical to draw a random sample of individuals from an entire population. But other experts criticized the *Lancet* authors for using too few. "I wouldn't survey a junior high school, no less an entire country, using only 47 cluster points," said Steven Moore, a Republican consultant who had conducted polling in Iraq for Coalition forces. One of the *Lancet* authors, Gilbert Burnham, replied that "surveying more clusters would have also meant more risk to the survey team." He said, "Had we used 470 clusters, our range of plausible values would have been about 3 times narrower." It is also possible that the results would have been far different.

Indeed, a survey of Iraq by the United Nations Development Programme used 2,200 cluster points, compared to only 33 used by the first *Lancet* study conducted four months later. And the study— *Iraq Living Conditions Survey 2004*—estimated only 24,000 deaths, roughly one quarter as many as *The Lancet* estimated at the time.

CONVERGENCE	In Chapter 6 we mentioned the notion of convergent evidence, and said that when different

methods arrive at similar estimates, those estimates are more credible. The reverse is also true: when results diverge, we should be more cautious. To be sure, the *Lancet* studies seem to support each other, but both produced results that are far higher than those of others. The Iraq Body Count project, for example, tabulated in November 2006 that between 47,016 and 52,142 deaths had been reported in Iraqi and international news media as a result of the 2003 invasion and the continuing violence. That's just 7 to 8 percent of *The Lancet*'s 654,965 figure published the previous month. It's true that the IBC estimates almost certainly missed some deaths that weren't reported, but we judge it unlikely that they could miss so many.

The 2004 *Lancet* study was inconsistent both with the Iraq Body Count tabulations and with the United Nations survey. Shortly after *The Lancet* had estimated 98,000 war deaths, the Iraq Body Count put the count between 14,619 and 16,804 as of December 7, 2004. The United Nations survey estimates war deaths at between 18,000 and 29,000, with the midpoint of that range at 24,000.

After the second *Lancet* study, Iraq Body Count officials issued a "reality check," disputing it and pointing out inconsistencies with other data. Delving into the details, they said that if the *Lancet* study was valid it would mean, among other improbabilities, that an average of 1,000 Iraqis had been killed by violence every single day in the first half of 2006, but that only one of those killings in ten had been noticed by any public surveillance mechanism. They said it also would mean 800,000 Iraqis suffered blast wounds or other serious conflict-related injuries over the preceding two years and that 90 percent of them went unnoticed by hospitals.

We can't say the *Lancet* studies are wrong. Unlike Mitch Snyder's "meaningless" estimate of 3 million homeless persons, which we discussed in Chapter 6, the *Lancet* estimates both were derived using scientifically accepted methods and were published in a reputable, peer-reviewed journal. The findings also are stoutly defended not only by the authors but by some independent experts as well. Nevertheless, given both the extraordinary imprecision of the figures and their failure to square with other observations, we can't accept them as accurate until and unless validated by other researchers using a much larger sample.

FINAL RULE: *Be Skeptical, but Not Cynical*

THE SKEPTIC DEMANDS EVIDENCE, AND RIGHTLY SO. THE CYNIC assumes that what he or she is being told is false. Throughout this book we've been urging you to be skeptical of factual claims, to demand and weigh the evidence and to keep your mind open. But too many people mistake cynicism for skepticism. Cynicism is a form of gullibility—the cynic rejects facts without evidence, just as the naïve person accepts facts without evidence. And deception born of cynicism can be just as costly or potentially as dangerous to health and well-being as any other form of deception.

To understand this notion, consider Kevin Trudeau, the author of a book that topped the *New York Times* best-seller list for a time in the summer of 2005: *Natural Cures "They" Don't Want You to Know About.* Trudeau pumped up sales with a massive campaign of late-night infomercials in which he claimed that "there are in fact natural, non-drug, and non-surgical cures for virtually every disease." His basic claim—an appeal to cynicism that he repeated over and over—was that "they" were conspiring to suppress information about known cures: "The drug companies don't want you to know the truth, the Food and Drug Administration, the U.S. government does not want you to know the truth. Why? Because it would cost them too much money in profits if you knew the inexpensive, natural remedies."

Trudeau's pitch is that "they" are lying but *he* will tell you the truth. Just buy his $14.95 book ($39.95 on audio CDs,) or subscribe to his $71.40-a-year newsletter, or become a $999 "lifetime member." And, oh, yes, buy his $19.95 weight-loss CD, whose title is, he claims, "censored by the Federal Trade Commission." Did you know the FTC is in on the conspiracy, too? As is the food industry, which, Trudeau claims, is putting unspecified ingredients in "diet" products that actually make people fat. No wonder we can't lose weight! The "censored" title: *How to Lose 30 Pounds in 30 Days,* just the sort of extravagant and unsupported claim the FTC often cites as misleading advertising.

We call Trudeau's pitch an appeal to cynicism because he is trading on the public's belief the federal government can't be trusted, and that big corporations—especially pharmaceutical companies—pursue profit so blindly that they are capable of almost any villainy. We might agree that some of the practices of drug companies justify criticism, but Trudeau is hoping you will automatically—cynically—accept his claim that big companies and the government are secretly conspiring to make you fat. This tactic has made untold millions of dollars for him, unless he's conning the public about that, too. His company once claimed to have sold 4 million copies of his book alone. His marketing plan must still be working, because in May 2006 he came out with a sequel: *More Natural Cures Revealed: Previously Censored Brand Name Products That Cure Disease.*

But here's why you should be skeptical—of Trudeau. Just do a little research using any Internet search engine and you will quickly discover a few facts about this master salesman:

- Trudeau has a criminal past. He served nearly two years in federal prison after a 1991 guilty plea to credit card fraud in which he bilked American Express of $122,735.68. In 1990, he served twenty-one days in jail and got a three-year suspended sentence on a Massachusetts state conviction for larceny after depositing $80,000 of worthless checks. At the time, he was posing as a doctor.

- Trudeau has been repeatedly cited for false advertising. In 1998, he agreed to pay $500,000 to settle

FTC charges that he appeared in a string of infomercials that claimed, among other things, that his "Mega Memory System" could enable anyone to achieve a photographic memory. In 2003, the FTC and FDA charged him with falsely claiming in infomercials that a dietary supplement called Coral Calcium Supreme could cure cancer. He agreed to stop making such claims but then continued to do so anyway, leading a federal judge in Chicago to find him in contempt of court. Later in 2004, Trudeau agreed to pay $2 million to the FTC and to cease making infomercials selling any product at all, except for "informational" material, which is protected by the First Amendment. That was when he switched from selling pills to selling books, CDs, and newsletters.

The $2.5 million that Trudeau has paid to settle earlier false-advertising cases is probably chump change compared to what he's taking in from a public made gullible by its own cynicism. It is easy to see why Trudeau's appeal works so well. Politicians love to blame "corporate greed" whenever prices go up, and Hollywood loves to cast corporate executives as villains in movies and TV crime shows. Since the Watergate scandals and the Vietnam War, a large majority of Americans who once trusted government to do the right thing now say they believe it is controlled by special interests and not run for the common benefit. Public trust of drug companies is particularly low. But that shouldn't be a reason to fall for the unsupported claims of a convicted felon and incorrigible huckster who's making millions selling books about bogus "natural cures." And anyone who tries using those "cures" instead of seeking competent medical advice is putting his or her health and even life at risk.

So we say cynicism can kill you. But you can save money, and maybe your life, if you are skeptical about claims like those made by Trudeau and the many others like him. Always look for real evidence.

Conclusion

Staying unSpun

STAYING UNSPUN REALLY BOILS DOWN TO FOLLOWING A FEW PRIN-
ciples that we've been talking about throughout this book. When
confronted with a claim, keep an open mind, ask questions, cross-
check, look for the best information, and then weigh the evidence.

CASE STUDY: *Hoodia Hoodoo*

TO SHOW HOW TO PUT THESE SIMPLE BUT POWERFUL MENTAL HAB-
its into practice, let's walk through a quick fact-checking of a real-
life claim you may already have encountered. Let's say you have
seen on the CBS News website a snippet of a *60 Minutes* program
in which correspondent Lesley Stahl is telling you about the next
big thing in dieting: a rare South African cactus called Gordon's

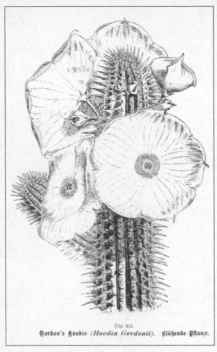

Gordon's Hoodia *(Hoodia Gordonii).* Glühende Pflanze.

Hoodia gordonii, the rare South African cactus purported to suppress appetite naturally

Hoodia (or *Hoodia gordonii*). Stahl is in the Kalahari Desert, where she says the native San tribespeople eat Hoodia to suppress their appetite on hunting trips. "Scientists say it fools the brain by making you think you're full, even if you've just eaten a morsel." A weight-loss pill may soon be on the market. The Web version of the story carries the headline "African Plant May Help Fight Fat: Lesley Stahl Reports on Newest Weapon in War on Obesity."

This is no late-night infomercial huckster talking; this is a tough reporter who once covered President Richard Nixon's Watergate scandal. Stahl reports that after eating a piece of the plant she went all day without feeling hungry, and that she experienced no aftereffects either. "I'd have to say it did work," she reports.

Wow! Where can I get this stuff? You quickly search the Internet for "hoodia," and find a cyber-bazaar of merchants hawking "Pure Hoodia," "Pure Hoodia Plus," "Hoodia Supreme," "Desert Burn" Hoodia, and any number of other brands. You also see websites offering advice on finding the "best" Hoodia products among all the clamoring competitors. Several provide a link to a video clip from the *60 Minutes* program on the CBS News website. They feature testimonials—for example, one from "Sarah" of Los Angeles, who says, "I used to always have cravings at night, but those cravings went away." This is sounding better and better.

But before you send off $149.95 for a five-month supply of this magical substance, take a few minutes to ask questions. How do I know this works, and is it safe? Just because Lesley Stahl swears by the freshly cut cactus she nibbled in the Kalahari Desert doesn't mean the capsules you buy from an Internet merchant will have the same effect, or even came from the same plant. And we had better dismiss those Internet testimonials: they're anecdotes at best, and they could be fabricated for all we know. Where are the scientific test results?

A bit of cross-checking turns up more information. Our Internet search has also brought up a 2003 story from a BBC reporter, Tom Mangold, who sampled the "Kalahari diet" even before Stahl. After eating a piece of cactus about half the size of a banana, Mangold reported that he and his cameraman "did not even think about food" for the four-hour drive back to Cape Town. "Dinnertime came and went. We reached our hotel at about midnight and went to bed without food. And the next day, neither of us wanted nor ate breakfast." But read on.

The BBC story also warns us that the stuff we've been seeing advertised may be just another weight-loss scam. The rights to develop a diet drug from Hoodia are owned by a British company named Phytopharm, and clinical trials still have several years to run. The reporter adds: "And beware Internet sites offering Hoodia 'pills' from the U.S., as we tested the leading brand and discovered it has no discernible Hoodia in it." Oddly, several Hoodia hucksters actually post a link to this BBC story on their websites, probably figuring that few will actually read it and most will just assume it's an endorsement.

To be fair to CBS, Stahl's full report also warned against the claims of Internet marketers of Hoodia products. It mentioned that the wild cactus is so rare that Phytopharm has established a plantation in an attempt to grow it in the huge quantities that would be required to meet demand should tests prove that the product is safe and effective. But the Internet Hoodia merchants who link to the CBS report probably figure you won't notice that part. They just post a link to the story, with introductions such as "Leslie [*sic*] Stahl . . . Hoodia works!!"

The BBC and CBS news stories—read in full—provide pretty strong warnings about the stuff being sold on the Web, but they are still secondhand sources. We can do better. On the Phytopharm website, we read, "The necessary clinical trials and other studies to ensure the safety of the [Hoodia] extract will take a few years before a product will be available." The site says that the company is just starting those trials, in collaboration with its partner Unilever. That tells us that this diet drug is far from ready for market.

At Phytopharm's site we also look for the "clinical study" conducted by the company in 2001 and mentioned in news reports and on many of the Hoodia websites. There is no report published in a medical journal—just a news release. It says the company ran a test of nineteen overweight men, giving half of them their patented "P57" Hoodia extract for fifteen days, while the other half got a placebo. The group getting P57 were said to have "a statistically significant decrease in daily calorie intake," a reduction of as much as 1,000 calories per day. We also learn from reading the company's press releases that before it hooked up with Unilever it had a deal with Pfizer to develop a commercial product from P57, but Pfizer backed out of the deal in 2003. Why would a major company drop a miracle weight-loss drug if it really had promise?

We've scouted up all this information for free, in a few minutes. For a small fee, you could have read on the *Consumer Reports* website an article briefly summarizing some of what we've said here, stating that there's "very scanty" evidence that Hoodia works, and concluding that "we do not recommend taking these supplements." (For $26 a year, we consider a subscription to *Consumer Reports* magazine and the website to be a bargain.)

When we weigh this evidence, we find that there's good reason to ignore the Hoodia hype, at least for now. Our TV correspondents, Stahl and Mangold, both gave us impressive anecdotal accounts of eating fresh cactus, but we won't find any of that at the supermarket. A British company, reputable enough to have partnered first with Pfizer and currently with Unilever, says we won't be able to buy their product for years. What's being offered for sale in the United States is claimed to be the cactus in powdered form, but we have no reliable way of knowing whether it's really Hoodia or just sawdust, or—more important—whether Hoodia powder works like fresh Hoodia. The testimonials we see on sellers' websites should be disregarded: we don't know who these people are, whether they really lost weight, or whether, if they did lose weight, the loss resulted from the pills. Furthermore, we have little idea of what harm these products might cause. Phytopharm's test group included only nineteen males. What if women took it? What if one person in every thousand experiences a life-threatening reaction? What happens if people take it for six months instead of just two weeks? Does it cause liver damage? What if Phytopharm sponsored other studies that produced less impressive results, and hasn't released them? We don't know.

Respect for Facts

We're not surprised that advertisers and politicians try to deceive us. Who can blame them for fabricating, twisting, exaggerating, or distorting the facts when we customers and citizens reward them so regularly with our money and votes? We should know that products like "Exercise in a Bottle" or Internet-advertised Hoodia won't make fat melt away without effort on our part. We even joke about how untrustworthy politicians are when they seek our votes. And yet enough people buy the products and the candidates to make all the spinning pay off.

These hucksters and partisans may not even realize how badly they are misleading us. Quite often, they seem to believe their own spin, even when a bit of rudimentary fact-checking shows it to be distorted or false. Remember the "your brain on politics" scans? In true believers, the portions of the brain used in rational thought just didn't light up. But from the consumer's standpoint—or the voter's— it doesn't matter whether the deception and spinning are deliberate. Either way, getting the facts wrong can cause us to waste six bucks on a cold remedy that may not work, or cause us to cheer for a war that doesn't look like such a good idea once we find out our leaders got the basic facts wrong.

So what can we do? Certainly an ordinary citizen can't be expected to outguess the CIA about the secret military capabilities of foreign nations. And maybe it's no big tragedy if we overpay for beauty products that don't really make wrinkles disappear. Indeed, maybe just thinking that wrinkles are gone is worth the money to some, and they might not mind being deceived. But generally, we're better off getting facts right, and we should try to get them right as consistently as we can.

Our advice boils down to two words: respect facts.

You'll be money ahead, for one thing. A little fact-checking is often all it takes to expose the advertising hype of an emu-oil saleswoman, a "clinically proven" cold remedy that isn't really proven, or an ex-con selling a book about cancer cures on late-night infomercials.

You'll save yourself time and annoyance if you develop the habits of mind we have recommended here. Respect for facts means keeping your mind engaged, so you won't fall for the next psychology student who cuts in line at the copy machine with a nonreason like "I have to make some copies," or for the many other nonreasons and the bogus logic that we're confronted with every day. Respect for facts also means checking your own assumptions. You could live years longer if you are a woman who respects the facts about what most women really die of, and then follows the medical advice that reduces those risks. You could avoid dying young if you are a teenager who respects the fact that teen drivers are four times more likely than older drivers to crash. Most teens don't; they tend to rate their own skills higher than those of their peers.

When it comes to politics, you can have the satisfaction of knowing you chose your candidate on the basis of facts, not just TV-spot fantasies. It might not change the way you vote, but then again, it might. Either way, you can be more confident you've made the right choice.

A greater respect for facts among our leaders could well have avoided a protracted and bloody war in Iraq. CIA officials failed to practice active open-mindedness, while the president and his top advisers pushed for evidence that would confirm their assumptions, not for evidence that might disprove them and show war to be unnecessary. The opposition showed little respect for facts as well: only half a dozen senators and a handful of House members even bothered to read the full National Intelligence Estimate prior to voting to authorize force. *The New York Times* apologized in 2004 for failing to report more skeptically in the months before the war.

We don't expect that one voter will change the way presidents or CIA directors or news organizations do their jobs. We don't expect that a single customer can bring about an end to bogus sales pitches. However, we do think that a movement of citizens can change these things. Start with the little things, such as what cold remedy to buy. Practice the habits of mind and the fact-checking skills we've suggested here. Apply those methods to more important matters. Then demand better. Don't reward those who disrespect facts, by buying their products or by voting for them. Do insist that they respect facts, respect you, and respect your intelligence and good sense. If enough of us do that, we believe that eventually our leaders will follow. When a group you support gets something wrong, speak up and ask them to correct it, as many NARAL supporters did when their group ran that ad we mentioned falsely accusing John Roberts of endorsing violence. If all sides in the political debate did that, the quality of discussion would rise.

You think our theory is goofy? It's up to you to show us the evidence. Try what we're suggesting. Prove us wrong.

Acknowledgments

A jointly authored book is invariably written in the voice of one of its authors. In academic circles, at least, that person's name appears first on the title page. The lead author is usually the one who has done the heavy lifting on the project, as well. Both are the case with *unSpun*. As the second author, I can certify both of those statements as fact.

Although not unheard-of, collaboration between an academic and a veteran of a wire service (The Associated Press), a major newspaper (*The Wall Street Journal*), and cable news (CNN) is a bit unusual. We are not sure how it works, and on most days are at least somewhat surprised that it does. Reducing the collaboration to its essence, Brooks brings to this book (and to FactCheck.org, which he directs) a nose for news, a talent for crafting fluent prose on deadline, and a desire to write on or near the Chesapeake Bay; I bring bibliographies of scholarly studies, a passing knowledge of how ads deceive, and an eagerness to add cryptic notes to anything Brooks has written. And we share the belief that Signe Wilkinson is an editorial cartoonist par excellence.

Brooks and I cooked up the idea of FactCheck.org out of our common concern about the seeming demise of fact in politics and out of respect for the deadlines and day-to-day pressures of journalism that make it difficult for reporters in already overstretched and understaffed media outlets to take on the task. We decided to write *unSpun* because we both believe that smart, informed citizens know some important things about detecting deception that can be captured in book form.

The third person on our team is Signe Wilkinson, who not only created the cartoons that you see throughout the book but also acted as our designated critic-in-chief. The fourth is our Random House editor, Tim Bartlett. Tim, who edited an earlier book of Kathleen's, both broadened the scope of *unSpun* and pruned its length. And he summoned more patience that any author can reasonably expect of an editor as we slowed the march of the book toward publication by pleading for the time to put it through an additional revision.

We are grateful as well to the FactCheck.org team in D.C., including Justin Bank, James Ficaro (who migrated to Philadelphia for law school), and Emi Kolawole, and to Miriam White, Jeff Gottfried, and Josh Gesell at the Annenberg Policy Center office in Philadelphia for sourcing and giving everything a second and sometimes third check. Emi in particular deserves our thanks for the endless hours she spent reviewing each word of the book for factual accuracy. Her work kept a number of errors from making their way into print. Any that remain are our responsbility alone. We also thank Jolanta Benal, whose uncommon attention to detail demonstrated that good copy editing is not a lost art after all.

Finally, we couldn't have written this book without the indulgence of the two to whom we dedicate it: Bev, who has put up with Brooks for nearly thirty-four years, and Bob, who has done the same with me for just over thirty-eight. And in a world of competing claims, that one is a certain fact.

KATHLEEN HALL JAMIESON
Philadelphia
October 2006

To what Kathleen says I would add this: I am grateful to her for allowing me the honor of being "lead" author on this book, but it has been a true collaboration. The words here are mostly mine, but the thoughts and ideas expressed here come from many months of talking and messaging between the two of us. Many of them, and perhaps most, would never have occurred to me working alone.

BROOKS JACKSON
California, Maryland
January 2007

SOURCES

To make this book as easy to read as possible, we've mostly omitted formal footnotes, end notes, and appendixes giving full details on the source of each fact or quote. We believe most of our sources are clearly stated in the text of the book. For those wishing more formal, academic sourcing, however, a full set of footnotes may be found at www.FactCheck.org/unSpun. We will also attempt to post on that site any relevant updates, clarifications, or (should the need arise) corrections.

blaming, spin and, 37–39
blogs, 69, 86, 141–43, 144
Blumenthal, Sidney, 37–38
Borenstein, Severin, 8
Boswell, James, 158
Bosworth, Barry, 14
Bradley, Bill, 149
Brady Campaign, 125
brain scans, biases and, 74, 75, 81,
   184
Brehm, Jack, 78
Bremer, L. Paul, 169
Britain, election ads of 2005 in, 57
Bryan, William Jennings, 155
Bullock, Daniel, 83–85
Bureau of Labor Statistics (BLS), ix, 14,
   121, 140, 159
Burnham, Gilbert, 173
Burt, Martha, 112–13
Bush, George H. W., 52, 53, 60, 98, 120,
   122
Bush, George W.
   "assault weapon ban" and, 44
   bin Laden family flight and, 17–19
   in campaign of 2000, 72–73
   in campaign of 2004, x, 7, 12, 31–32,
      37, 39, 57, 72
   deficit spending and, 36, 163
   as forty-third president, 162–63
   Iraq War and, 27–28, 36, 54, 156,
      161, 170–71, 172
   judicial nominees of, 165
   New Orleans flooding and, 37–38
   "Orwellian" language and, 48
   September 11 attack and, 128, 129
   Texas Air National Guard and, 142
   visual backdrops and, 53–54
   on White House website, 135
Bush, George W., administration
   abortion statistics and, 116–18
   drinking water standards and, 32–33
   economic statistics and, viii–ix, 11–13,
      56, 163
   energy policies of, 7–8
   environmental record of, 34
   estate taxes and, 113, 114
   Hurricane Katrina aftermath and,
      37–38
   Social Security and, 20, 47–48, 57–58,
      72–73
   tax cuts and, 39–40, 48, 55, 56
Bush, Laura, 91–92

campaigns, presidential, 22–23, 52–53,
   57, 71, 95, 122
   of 2000, 72–73
   of 2004, x, 5, 7, 11–18, 23, 31–32, 33,
      39–40, 44–45, 72, 75, 122, 123
   See also names of candidates
Canada, 8, 20
cancer
   quack cures for, 87–89, 120, 177, 184
   reliable information on, 122
   in women, 89–92
Cantril, Hadley, 74–75
Carson, Clayborne, 150
Casey, Robert, 73
Castro, Fidel, 60
Census Bureau, U.S., ix, 112, 134, 140
Center for Responsive Politics, 139, 165
Centers for Disease Control and
   Prevention (CDC), 10–11, 118, 139
Central Intelligence Agency (CIA), 16,
   60, 61, 67, 77, 96, 156–57, 184,
   185
Cheney, Dick, 12, 61, 161
Chin, Denny (U.S. District Court
   judge), 10
choices, rationalization of, 78–79
Clausewitz, Carl von, 100
Cleveland, Grover, 163
Clinton, Bill, 57, 58–59, 60, 149, 161
Clinton administration, xi, 32–33, 34,
   44–45, 56
"close call," psychology of, 78–79
cognitive dissonance, 67, 69
Cold-Eeze, 118–20, 122, 184
commercials. See advertising, deceptive;
   political advertising
Community for Creative Non-Violence
   (CCNV), 110–11
comparative terms, spin and, 31–33
confessions, as evidence, 170–71
Confessions of an Advertising Man
   (Ogilvy), 20
confirmation bias, 76–78, 81
   See also partisanship; stereotyping
Congress, U.S., Internet resources on,
   135–36, 139, 143
Congressional Budget Office (CBO), 36,
   37, 114, 136, 139
Consumer Reports magazine, 87, 139, 182
"convergent evidence," 113, 169, 173–75
Cooper, Frank, 99
cosmetics, advertising for, 4–5, 50, 184

About the Authors

BROOKS JACKSON runs the Annenberg Public Policy Center's award-winning website FactCheck.org and was an investigative reporter for The Associated Press, *The Wall Street Journal,* and CNN. He is the author of *Honest Graft: Big Money and the American Political Process* and *Broken Promise: Why the Federal Election Commission Failed.* He lives in Washington, D.C.

KATHLEEN HALL JAMIESON is the Elizabeth Ware Packard Professor of Communication and director of the Annenberg Public Policy Center of the University of Pennsylvania. She is the author or co-author of eleven books, including *Dirty Politics: Deception, Distraction, and Democracy, Packaging the Presidency,* and *The Press Effect.*